COMPLEX PTSD WORKBOOK

10 Ways to Get Your Sh*T Together

TABLE OF CONTENTS

Introduction 1

Chapter 1: Kicking the Numbing Habit: Ditch the Dependencies and Face the Feelings 5

    Recognizing Unhealthy Coping Mechanisms 6

    The Dangers of Numbing Emotional Pain 8

    Embracing Your Feelings and Emotions 11

    Healthy Alternatives for Coping With Pain 15

    The Role of Professional Help in Breaking Dependencies 17

Chapter 2: Therapeutic Trust: Building a Rock-Solid Relationship with Your Therapist 19

    Understanding the Unique Challenges in Therapeutic Relationships 20

    Establishing Trust and Safety in Therapy 21

    Effective Communication With Your Therapist 23

    Managing Emotions During Therapy Sessions 25

    Collaborating for a Successful Recovery Journey 27

Chapter 3: Anchoring to the Now: Stop Time-Traveling and Embrace the Present 29

    The Pitfalls of Living in the Past or Future 29

    Cultivating Mindfulness for Self-Awareness 31

    Techniques for Staying Present and Engaged 33

    Overcoming External Validation Seeking 35

    The Power of Embracing the Present Moment 36

Chapter 4: Identity Makeover: Uncover the Real You Beyond Trauma ... 39

    The Struggle to Find Identity After Trauma 40

    Strategies for Personal Growth and Self-Discovery 41

    Building Resilience for a Stronger Sense of Self 43

Redefining Your Values and Beliefs 45

Embracing the Journey of Self-Exploration 47

Chapter 5: UIT the Blame Game: Own Your Healing and Thrive 50

The Trap of Blaming Others 51

Taking Responsibility for Your Healing Journey 52

Shifting Focus to Personal Growth and Accountability 56

Letting Go of Resentment and Anger 57

Embracing Empowerment in Recovery 59

Chapter 6: No ≠ Abandonment: Decode Rejection and Keep Calm 61

Understanding the Fear of Abandonment in c-PTSD 61

Tools for Recognizing and Managing Emotional Responses 63

Developing Healthier Interpretations of Rejection 65

Building Self-Awareness and Emotional Regulation 67

Fostering Secure and Fulfilling Relationships 69

Chapter 7: Sensitivity Takedown: Stay Cool in
the Heat of Social Encounters 72

Interpersonal Hypersensitivity and c-PTSD 72

Coping Strategies for Managing Emotional Reactions 74

Navigating Social Situations With Confidence 75

Strengthening Emotional Boundaries 76

Building a Supportive Social Network 78

Chapter 8: Smash Self-Sabotage: Dare to Embrace
Change and Success 80

Identifying Self-Sabotaging Behaviors 81

Challenging Fears of Change and Success 84

Embracing Growth and Progress in Recovery 87

Celebrating Your Achievements and Milestones 89

Chapter 9: Emotional Tightrope: Balance Oversharing and Authenticity Like a Pro 91

Understanding the Struggle to Find Balance in Relationships 92

Strategies for Modifying Oversharing Behaviors 93

Developing Healthy Boundaries and Emotional Regulation 94

Enhancing Interpersonal Skills and Communication 95

Fostering Authentic Connections 97

Chapter 10: Bye-Bye Comparison: Hello Self-Compassion and Personal Growth 99

The Pitfalls of Constant Comparison 100

Focusing on Personal Growth and Self-Compassion 101

Cultivating a Productive and Positive Mindset in Recovery 102

Strategies for Overcoming the Comparison Trap 104

Embracing Your Unique Journey and Successes 106

Chapter 11: Rise From the Ashes: Gig-Work Your Way to Self-Sufficiency and Confidence 108

B.1 The Hopelessness, Helplessness, and Unemployment Trap 108

B.2 Cultivating Self-Sufficiency for Recovery 110

B.3 Developing a Sense of Purpose and Direction 111

B.4 Strategies for Gaining Confidence and Employability 112

B.5 Balancing Work, Relationships, and Self-Care for a Stronger Recovery 114

Conclusion 116

Description 121

INTRODUCTION

Welcome to the Complex PTSD Workbook, where we will explore ways to help you understand complex PTSD and to give you skills that can help you better manage your trauma symptoms. If you're reading this, chances are you've experienced some form of trauma that has left you feeling overwhelmed, anxious, and unable to cope with day-to-day challenges. You're not alone--over 22% of adults and 20% of children have experienced some form of trauma. Many people who have experienced trauma struggle with PTSD, but there is a less commonly recognized condition called complex post-traumatic stress disorder (C-PTSD). This workbook is designed to help you gain skills to manage your symptoms better and improve your everyday life, no matter what those symptoms are. You may have been told that there's no "magic pill" to fix your problems, but I promise there are many things that you can learn that will improve your life.

Complex PTSD, or C-PTSD, is a form of post-traumatic stress disorder resulting from prolonged exposure to trauma, such as childhood abuse, domestic violence, or military combat. It can lead to various symptoms, including hypervigilance, emotional dysregulation, and difficulty forming and maintaining healthy relationships. C-PTSD is very common and can affect anyone who has experienced traumatic experiences. However, a lack of self-awareness and misperceptions about what's happening can hurt people with C-PTSD and make them feel alone in their struggle. This is where the Complex PTSD Workbook comes in. I am here to help you learn tools to better cope with C-PTSD symptoms and improve your life.

Complex PTSD is often first seen in adults. It can affect many areas of life, including your job or career, your relationship with family members or friends, and even how you cope with everyday life. You might be able to experience Complex PTSD on your own, but if you need professional help - some common treatments for Complex PTSD can help you.

Complex PTSD doesn't only affect adults; children and teens can experience this disorder in its many forms. Children cannot understand what they're going through and may need professional assistance when recovering from their trauma, like adult patients who have undergone treatment for Complex PTSD.

Many PTSD symptoms are treatable, but you must try to do so. Many people with PTSD have been told their symptoms were "normal" and "expected" of them - and as a result, they feel overwhelmed and exhausted from handling the constant demands of dealing with trauma. This workbook will help you identify your symptoms, learn about treatments that can help relieve your symptoms, and even find ways to live with some peace of mind.

Throughout this book, you will find numerous self-care techniques that will help you improve your coping skills. You will learn what helps you cope with certain triggers and how to deal with them calmly and nonviolently. You will learn how to take care of yourself and set limits on your symptoms to better manage the stressors in your life. I hope this workbook will help you find a way to restore some of the self-awareness and peace of mind you've lost from coping with complex PTSD.

Be forewarned: becoming a better person doesn't happen overnight, but there are many things you can do to become more "normal" in your daily life. You may have heard people say that "you can't always be normal" because sometimes normal involves caring for others and having time for hobbies or hobbies. Sometimes, many people will tell you that it's not "normal" to take care of yourself. This is why it's so important to be kind to yourself - and learn good self-care techniques in healing.

Complex PTSD is a serious condition that can leave you feeling helpless and overwhelmed. But I'm here to tell you there is hope. Many tools and tools can help make your symptoms more manageable so that you can find ways to cope with your triggers without them becoming overwhelming or difficult for you to manage. This workbook will provide exercises and activities that will help restore some peace of mind and skills that will help you cope with the symptoms of complex PTSD in the future.

Many people have PTSD. It can be difficult to recover from this disorder and take control of your life. This workbook offers a way of understanding the stages many go through when dealing with trauma and how to avoid those stages when possible. The workbook is a collection of 10 steps which starts by acknowledging what the person has done wrong, then moves on to accepting responsibility for mistakes and feelings, finding peace in forgiveness and love, coping with triggers in healthy ways, being present for yourself through meditation or exercise, enjoying nature as therapy without leaving home or going out of your way; getting control over negative thoughts by developing positive self-talk; strengthening positive networks as you reintegrate into society; developing strategies for success by planning. The workbook contains helpful strategies, examples, and resources for each step.

This self-help book does not attempt to replace professional help. If you need therapy, find a therapist now. The book can be used as a companion to therapy or an adjunct to medication. It can also be used by people who are not currently in therapy or taking medication. Still, it could benefit from an organized recovery system for PTSD.

The workbook offers hope and encouragement for the road ahead without excuses or a victim mentality. This book contains practical ideas, step-by-step habit-building techniques, emotional release techniques, and more. Although written from a victim's perspective, many concepts can apply to trauma survivors or people who struggle with PTSD.

This workbook will explore strategies for helping you move forward on your healing journey. These strategies are based on the latest research in trauma recovery and have been proven effective in helping individuals with C-PTSD.

So, whether you're just starting your journey or looking for new ways to enhance your recovery, this workbook supports you. Remember, healing from trauma is a process that takes time and effort. But with commitment and perseverance, you can overcome your challenges and create the life you deserve.

CHAPTER 1

KICKING THE NUMBING HABIT: DITCH THE DEPENDENCIES AND FACE THE FEELINGS

This refers to breaking free from behaviors or substances used to avoid or numb unpleasant emotions, memories, or sensations. This numbing habit can be developed in response to trauma or difficult life circumstances.

Numbing is a common coping mechanism used by individuals who have experienced trauma or difficult life circumstances. It involves using substances, behaviors, or activities to avoid or numb unpleasant emotions, memories, or sensations. While numbing may provide temporary relief, it can ultimately lead to more significant problems and hinder healing. If you're struggling with numbing habits, it's essential to recognize that recovery is possible.

By facing their feelings, individuals can learn to manage their emotions healthily, build resilience, and heal from past trauma. This process often involves identifying the numbing habits, understanding the triggers that lead to their use, and developing alternative coping strategies such as exercise, meditation, or seeking professional help.

While breaking the numbing habit can be challenging, it is a crucial step in recovery. It can lead to a more fulfilling and meaningful life.

Recognizing Unhealthy Coping Mechanisms

Recognizing unhealthy coping mechanisms can be difficult and often takes time. Recognizing your numbing habits and what triggers them can help you adopt healthier ways of dealing with your emotions.

To recognize unhealthy coping mechanisms, you must try different approaches and notice the results for yourself. It may take a little time and patience, but if you remain committed, you'll soon be able to identify these habitual responses in yourself.

Unhealthy coping mechanisms are behaviors or actions that individuals use to deal with stress, difficult emotions, or life challenges in a way that can be harmful or detrimental to their overall well-being. These coping mechanisms can develop in response to trauma, abuse, or other challenging life circumstances. Often these coping mechanisms are not fully understood or recognized by the individual until they have reached a significant point of distress. It is important to realize that these behaviors are typically temporary and can become more complex the longer they persist.

While unhealthy coping mechanisms may seem harmless initially, they can have serious psychological and emotional consequences if left unchecked. In some instances, these behaviors can become compulsive or even destructive.

With treatment, unhealthy coping mechanisms can replace healthier thinking, feeling, and acting patterns that allow for a greater sense of well-being.

Here are some examples of unhealthy coping mechanisms:

a) Substance use: A common unhealthy coping mechanism for individuals experiencing trauma, abuse, or other difficult life circumstances, substance use is the consistent or chronic use of alcohol, illicit drugs, or prescription medications that helps to numb pain or distress.

b) Sexual behavior: Exploitive sexual behavior can be an unhealthy coping mechanism people develop in response to past trauma and other difficult life circumstances. This may include compulsive sex talk, excessive masturbation, compulsive cybersex, and seduction of others.

c) Self-medication: Self-medication is the inappropriate use of medication, illicit drugs, or prescription medications to relieve distress or deal with emotional pain.

d) Self-harm is the deliberate infliction of pain or injury on one's appearance or body.

e) Extreme exercise: Excessive exercise is an unhealthy coping mechanism for individuals who have experienced trauma or difficult life circumstances. It may involve overtraining, consuming stimulants, or developing a skewed body image.

f) Lying: Lying can be an unhealthy coping mechanism people develop in response to past trauma or other difficult life circumstances. Examples include lying to oneself and others, white lies, and exaggeration.

g) Avoidance: Avoiding situations or people that trigger negative emotions or memories can lead to isolation and social withdrawal.

h) Emotional eating: Using food to cope with difficult emotions can lead to unhealthy eating patterns and weight gain.
i) Procrastination: Avoiding important tasks or responsibilities to avoid stress or anxiety.
j) Denial: Refusing to acknowledge or accept negative emotions or difficult situations can lead to unresolved issues and emotional distress.
k) Compulsive behaviors: Engaging in repetitive behaviors or rituals to relieve anxiety or stress, such as excessive cleaning or checking.

It's important to recognize these unhealthy coping mechanisms and work to replace them with healthier alternatives. This can involve seeking professional help, developing new coping skills, or finding support from friends and family. Remember, recovery is possible, and with the right tools and support, individuals can overcome unhealthy coping mechanisms and lead healthier and happier lives.

The Dangers of Numbing Emotional Pain

Many individuals suffering from past trauma, abuse, or other difficult life circumstances have developed unhealthy coping mechanisms in response to stress and distress. These coping strategies may help them deal with their emotional pain in the short term, but they can be harmful and destructive in the long run.

Emotional pain is a normal part of life that everyone experiences occasionally. Our emotional responses to this pain differ from person to person.

While some individuals can cope with their distress and negative emotions using healthy responses and appropriate outlets, others may use unhealthy coping mechanisms when dealing with these feelings. Unfortunately, many unhealthy coping mechanisms can harm the individual and the surrounding individuals.

It is important to recognize the dangers of numbing emotional pain. While unhealthy coping mechanisms may initially help individuals cope with emotional pain and distress, they can lead to long-term consequences that damage their mental health.

Numbing emotional pain is a common coping mechanism used by individuals who have experienced trauma, abuse, or other difficult life circumstances. It involves using substances, behaviors, or activities to avoid or numb unpleasant emotions, memories, or sensations. While numbing may provide temporary relief, it can ultimately lead to more significant problems and hinder healing.

Here are some dangers of numbing emotional pain:

Increased emotional distress: By avoiding your feelings, you are simply postponing the inevitable. When you experience emotional pain and discomfort in the future, you will have no healthy outlets to deal with them. This can build up emotional distress, making it difficult to function or enjoy life.

Psychological dependence: You may feel trapped or trapped by emotions you cannot control, which can worsen your mental health.

Increased risk of addiction: Compulsive use of substances, behaviors, or activities may become more frequent due to numbing negative emotions.

This can lead to negative health consequences and increased potential for addiction.

Interpersonal problems: Avoiding emotions and not dealing with emotional pain can also lead to interpersonal problems, such as conflicts with family, friends, or romantic partners.

Mental health problems: Numbing emotional pain can contribute to mental health problems such as depression, anxiety, and post-traumatic stress disorder (PTSD).

Inability to heal: Avoiding emotions and not dealing with emotional pain can hinder the healing process and make it difficult for individuals to move forward from traumatic experiences.

Interpersonal and intercultural problems: Avoiding emotions and not dealing with emotional pain can lead to interpersonal and intercultural problems such as mistrust, deception, or disrespect.

Loss of trust: Numbing emotional pain can cause a loss of trust in family, friends, or others. This can lead to further emotional damage in the long term.

Disconnection from life: By numbing emotional pain, you may lose connection with life and become detached from the present moment. You may also lose positive aspects of your life and eventually become disconnected.

It's important to recognize the dangers of numbing emotional pain and work to replace unhealthy coping mechanisms with healthier alternatives. This can involve seeking professional help, developing new coping skills, or finding support from friends and family. Remember, healing from emotional pain is possible. With the right tools and support, individuals can lead fulfilling and meaningful lives.

Embracing Your Feelings and Emotions

With the right tools and support, healing from traumatic experiences, emotions, and behaviors that have damaged your mental health is possible. However, it is important to utilize a healthy approach that helps you embrace your feelings and emotions. Embracing your feelings and emotions will allow you to feel safe expressing and dealing with them healthily. Additionally, it allows you to communicate with others more effectively.

Here are some benefits of embracing your feelings and emotions:

Personal growth: Healing from traumas, abuse, or other difficult experiences can benefit personal growth. By opening up about these issues, individuals can gain insight into themselves and their lives that may lead them to change for the better.

Improved relationships: By embracing your feelings, you can open up to family, friends, and romantic partners. This improves your relationships with these individuals and helps you to heal in a safe environment.

Effective communication: By embracing your feelings and expressing them appropriately, you can communicate with family, friends, and loved ones in a constructive way that heals rather than damages relationships.

Improved mental health: Communicating openly about your emotions may help you cope better with painful memories or experiences, causing improvement in your mental health.

Enhanced emotional well-being: Individuals can feel more contentment with their lives by directly experiencing and expressing previously numbed or suppressed emotions.

Stress relief: When you embrace and express your feelings appropriately, you can release emotional tension that may build up over time.

Improved emotional intelligence: By embracing your feelings, you can learn better to understand your emotions and those of others. This can help you improve relationships and find success in a variety of situations.

Life enrichment: If embraced correctly, feelings such as sadness, grief, or anger can enhance life experience. They help individuals grow by exposing new possibilities they may have never experienced otherwise.

Positive self-image: Negative self-images may develop due to past trauma or abuse. However, it is possible to improve your self-image by embracing and healthily expressing your feelings.

Increased confidence: By embracing and expressing your feelings appropriately, you can gain self-confidence and learn to handle difficult situations.

To embrace your feelings and emotions healthily, it is helpful to communicate with others who have experienced similar experiences or have professional expertise on emotional trauma. Finding support from others as you begin to heal is also beneficial.

To help you embrace your feelings and emotions, here are some ways to improve communication:

    a) Be non-judgmental: Judgmental attitudes can make people feel that they are not being heard, leading them to avoid expressing feelings in the first place. By being non-judgmental, individuals can better communicate their emotions and healthily deal with them.

b) Explore feelings calmly: Having conversations about feelings calmly and composedly allows individuals to express themselves freely without judgment. When expressing emotions freely, individuals may become overwhelmed or experience anxiety, allowing them to step back and regain composure.

c) Remember difficult experiences: By remembering painful experiences, individuals can gain perspective and recognize that they have overcome these difficulties. This can help them cope better with present emotional situations.

d) Show empathy: When expressing feelings, it is important to show empathy to others. This allows them to feel heard and recognized for the emotional pain that they are experiencing.

e) Avoid criticizing others: Avoid criticizing them or their emotions when communicating about emotional issues. Instead, please help them to understand themselves better and the emotions that they are feeling.

f) Use "I" statements: Using "I" statements when expressing feelings allows individuals to maintain control over their emotions without making others feel judged or criticized.

g) Ask "why" questions: By asking "why" questions, individuals can better understand their feelings and identify the source of the pain. This helps them understand their feelings and find a healthy solution.

h) Take action: When expressing feelings and emotions, take action in a healthy way that is appropriate for you. For example, if you want to cry or release anger, do so in a safe manner that is appropriate for you.

i) Don't beat yourself up about painful memories: Avoid beating yourself up about the past. This can lead to future emotional issues and may prevent you from reaching your mental health goals. Instead, let go of painful memories by embracing your feelings and expressing them appropriately.

j) Remember feelings are temporary: Emotions come and go in life. When you experience an emotion, remember that it is temporary and can be released through rational thought processes or by letting it flow naturally.

k) Listen to music: Music can help you healthily express emotions by letting you let go of painful memories.

l) Trust your instincts: Our bodies and minds are naturally equipped to deal with emotions healthily when we trust our instincts or gut feeling. By trusting your instincts, you can communicate feelings properly without pent-up tension from the past getting in the way.

m) Do something you enjoy: You can release negative feelings and improve your mood by doing something you enjoy. Finding social outlets that allow you to do things with others as a way of expression is helpful.

n) Spend time with others: It is important to spend time with others healthily when seeking help from others for emotional trauma. Please encourage your friends and family members to help you embrace your emotions and express them appropriately.

o) Regular exercise can help the body naturally release positive and negative emotions.

p) Accept progress: Avoid comparing yourself to others or feeling like you have failed if progress is not made quickly enough. Instead, accept that you are going at your own pace.

q) Avoid triggers: Our mind and body can become anxious when trapped or in danger. It is important to avoid environments that may trigger negative feelings in the future, such as places you do not feel safe or are not familiar with.

r) Highlight strengths: When experiencing a difficult situation, it is important to focus on your strengths and accomplishments to express feelings. Focusing on your strengths allows you to remain positive in the future and continue reaching your mental health goals.

Healthy Alternatives for Coping With Pain

To cope with emotional trauma and prevent issues from worsening, it is important to have healthy alternatives for dealing with stress. Instead of avoiding or denying problems, it is helpful to find healthy solutions so that individuals can implement a routine that allows them to relax and focus their energy on things they enjoy.

There are many different ways to cope with emotional trauma. To cope healthily, it is important to avoid high-risk behaviors such as self-injury or engaging in dangerous sexual activity. Instead of overindulging in alcohol and drugs as a way of distancing yourself from your emotions, try healthier alternatives like talking with friends and family members about what you are going through.

Individuals can also take action in their environment by identifying the causes of stress in their lives. Changing your environment will address the source of stress and help you feel better.

Suppose you are experiencing emotional trauma and do not know how to cope. In that case, seeking help from a mental health professional who can guide you toward healthier alternatives for coping with emotional trauma is important.

Finding healthy alternatives to cope with and manage those difficult emotions is important when dealing with emotional pain. Here are some healthy alternatives to numbing or avoiding emotional pain:

Exercise: Exercise can help reduce stress and release endorphins, natural mood boosters.

Mindfulness practices: Mindfulness practices such as meditation, deep breathing, or yoga can help calm the mind and reduce stress.

Journaling: Writing down your thoughts and feelings can help process difficult emotions and provide a sense of release.

Support groups: Joining a support group can provide a safe space to share experiences and connect with others who have gone through similar situations.

Therapy: Working with a therapist can help individuals process difficult emotions and develop healthy coping skills.

Hobbies: Engaging in hobbies or activities that bring joy and fulfillment can help reduce stress and provide a sense of purpose.

Self-care: Practicing self-care, such as taking a warm bath, getting a massage, or treating oneself to a favorite food, can provide comfort and care.

It's important to remember that healing from emotional pain takes time and effort. By incorporating healthy coping skills, individuals can learn to manage their emotions healthily and heal from past trauma.

The Role of Professional Help in Breaking Dependencies

Psychological trauma can become a significant issue in individuals who experience mental illness. For this reason, many seek professional help to break dependencies and address the underlying issues.

Professional help is important to break individuals' dependencies on drugs or alcohol, which are not healthy coping mechanisms for people with mental illnesses. To overcome issues related to addiction, it is important to seek professional assistance and learn how to avoid unhealthy coping mechanisms.

When seeking professional help, it's important to understand that therapists are trained professionals who can help identify and address underlying influences that lead to addiction. Ultimately, therapy focuses on learning healthier alternatives for managing emotions and breaking down unhealthy dependencies to maintain a healthy lifestyle in the future.

Breaking dependencies can be challenging, and professional help can be essential in supporting individuals in this journey. This is why seeking professional help is important if you are struggling with addiction.

Many professionals will encourage individuals to consider therapy as a way of breaking dependencies in the future. This may be in the form of individual or group counseling, or even the combination of both, to provide a wide range of support and guidance during treatment.

When seeking professional help for an addiction, it's important to find a therapist experienced in treating mental illness. Professionals who treat substance abuse tend to be less effective because they do not understand how mental illness can influence addictions.

When seeking professional help for an addiction, it's important to remember that you deserve support and a high level of care from professionals.

Professional help can provide a safe and supportive environment for individuals to address dependencies, learn new coping skills, and work toward long-term recovery. It's important to remember that breaking dependencies is a process and may involve setbacks. Still, with the right support and tools, individuals can overcome dependencies and lead healthier, happier lives.

CHAPTER 2

THERAPEUTIC TRUST: BUILDING A ROCK-SOLID RELATIONSHIP WITH YOUR THERAPIST

Therapeutic trust is a critical component of the therapeutic relationship between a therapist and a client. It is built on mutual respect, honesty, and empathy, essential for successful therapy outcomes. Therapeutic trust allows clients to disclose more of their secrets, share deeper and more personal information, and take risks needed to heal. When a therapeutic relationship is built on trust, the relationship can develop into a mutually supportive bond in which both therapist and client are dedicated to the same end goal—the betterment of the client.

For therapists, establishing therapeutic trust with clients is equally important. Therapists who build this type of trust model will be able to have an equal relationship with their clients, one in which all parties openly communicate about treatment goals, progress made toward these goals, and other factors that are important for both the client's success and satisfaction with the treatment process.

Building therapeutic trust takes time and effort, but it's worth it for its benefits to the therapeutic relationship and the healing process. By working collaboratively with your therapist and following these principles, you can build a rock-solid relationship based on trust, empathy, and respect.

Understanding the Unique Challenges in Therapeutic Relationships

Therapeutic relationships can be complex and challenging, involving individuals in vulnerable positions and dealing with difficult emotions and experiences. Building a therapeutic relationship that is stable and enduring can pose problems and obstacles for clients. Clients may have trust issues with their therapist, they may feel misunderstood, they may have misgivings about the treatment process, or they may be dealing with other stressful personal or emotional issues that affect the health of their mental health.

Clients may resist therapy for various reasons, such as fear of change or vulnerability. Resistance can make establishing rapport and trust in the therapeutic relationship challenging.

Therapeutic relationships involve ethical considerations, such as confidentiality and informed consent. Ethical dilemmas can arise in the therapeutic relationship and require attention and adherence to professional standards. Therapists also must balance the needs of clients who are actively engaging in treatment, as opposed to clients who need treatment as a safety net or whose symptoms have not improved.

Therapists, too, face unique challenges in therapeutic relationships. Therapists from other fields without much training in psychology face unique communication challenges with clients. Different cultures and backgrounds are also a source of unique challenges for therapists. Whatever the case, therapists who can tackle these issues head-on will be advantageous in building therapeutic trust over time.

Additionally, both clients and therapists may have differing expectations of what the outcome of treatment will be. Differences in goals and expectations may lead to problems in the therapeutic relationship if they aren't discussed openly and constructively. This can make it even more challenging for both parties to work together toward a common goal, which is essential for effective treatment.

Don't give up on treatment if you and your therapist have trouble collaborating effectively, getting stuck in cycles of avoidance or conflict, or experiencing empathy gaps or miscommunications. Instead, talk to your therapist about what you're feeling and whether you can do anything to improve the quality of the therapeutic relationship. Often, with a little effort on both parties' parts, these problems can be cleared up, and trust can be built.

Navigating these challenges requires awareness, communication, and ongoing attention to the therapeutic relationship. Therapists can establish a safe and supportive environment for healing and growth by working collaboratively and openly with their clients.

Establishing Trust and Safety in Therapy

A strong therapeutic relationship between you and the therapist is essential for full healing and healing outcomes. Trust is the foundation of a therapeutic relationship. Still, it cannot be easy to build when you first start seeing your therapist or if the therapeutic relationship has been going on for some time.

First, you have to decide whether you will trust your therapist. Suppose your feelings about therapy and what will happen during treatment are anxiety-provoking. In that case, you must contact your therapist as soon as possible and discuss how this may affect your ability to work cooperatively with them. If necessary, the two of you can devise a plan for easing into treatment and building trust before starting sessions.

Once you've decided to trust your therapist, it's important to establish a therapeutic relationship so that you both feel safe and comfortable. You should be able to ask your therapist questions without fear of judgment. You should also know where the boundaries of acceptable therapy lie and what types of personal information can be shared between you and your therapist. It would help if you had a say in the treatment process, including what treatment goals are set, when your sessions will occur, and anything important to know about the therapy experience.

Once you feel safe and comfortable in treatment, you can establish trust with your therapist. Trust is built through interactions between client and therapist in which both parties feel heard and understood; trust is reinforced as a result. Establishing therapeutic trust takes time. Emotions and experiences can be challenging to discuss openly; at first, it may be difficult to wrestle with complicated issues or share parts of yourself normally hidden from others. Your therapist will be working with you to help you open up and reveal these parts of yourself to each other.

When trust is built, it can help the therapeutic relationship endure even when difficult feelings and emotions arise, when mistakes are made, or when problems occur in the treatment process. However, dealing with these situations can be more difficult when trust is shaky.

Therapeutic trust is developed in three steps: establishing safety, sharing vulnerabilities, and building a connection or relationship. When you establish safety with your therapist, you feel that your therapist will accept whatever you have to say without judgment or criticism. You can also feel safe being honest about your problems and feelings.

Once you can talk freely with your therapist, you can share vulnerable parts of yourself, such as thoughts, feelings, and experiences. These things may not seem extremely important initially. Still, they're much harder to share when hidden and not something people usually discuss with their therapists. You can also get in touch with the good things during therapy sessions—when you feel understood by your therapist or respond well to a therapeutic intervention—and recall those moments to build trust.

Effective Communication With Your Therapist

Therapeutic communication is all about getting your message across to your therapist. Part of that is also about listening to what your therapist has to say, but first, let's talk about how you can effectively communicate with the people you see in therapy.

When communicating with a therapist, it helps if you make eye contact; look your therapist in the eyes and have them look back at you. It may be easier for some people than others, but if eye contact is difficult for you or makes you feel uncomfortable, then look away and talk while looking down or straight ahead. It's important to feel comfortable during counseling sessions to speak freely and get things off your chest.

In addition, most therapists give their clients a lot of freedom regarding how they speak during therapy sessions. If you are open and honest with the therapist, you will likely be able to connect. It's OK to be straightforward with your therapist. Still, if you find yourself overly critical or judgmental during sessions, it might help to tone down your language and avoid insulting or blaming others. Also, when speaking to a therapist, you mustn't give advice. This can be hard at first because it seems like something we want or expect from others. However, when people listen to advice givers, they often feel worse about themselves than before they started listening.

Be open and honest. Being open and honest with your therapist is essential, as they can only help you if they clearly understand your thoughts, feelings, and experiences. Avoid hiding information or downplaying your emotions, as this can hinder the therapeutic process.

Be specific. Try to be as specific as possible when discussing your concerns with your therapist. Rather than saying, "I feel anxious," try to identify specific triggers or situations that cause your anxiety.

Ask questions. Don't be afraid to ask your therapist questions about their approach, their qualifications, or any other concerns you may have. Asking questions can help you feel more comfortable and confident in your therapy sessions.

Provide feedback. If something your therapist says or doesn't feel helpful or comfortable with, constructively provide feedback. This can help improve the therapeutic relationship and ensure you get the needed support.

Using "I" statements can help you express your feelings without blaming or accusing others. For example, saying "I feel unsupported" rather than

"You're not supporting me" can be more effective in communicating your emotions.

Practice active listening. Active listening involves being fully present and engaged with your therapist. It can help you understand their perspective and get the most out of your therapy sessions.

Remember that therapy is a collaborative process, and effective communication is critical to achieving your goals. You can work with your therapist to create a supportive and effective therapeutic relationship by being open, specific, and honest.

Managing Emotions During Therapy Sessions

One of the most basic things you can do to help you get the most out of therapy is to learn skills for managing your emotions. Sometimes, you may feel sad, angry, frustrated, or anxious during sessions. It's important to know how to manage these emotions healthily.

Managing emotions during therapy sessions can be challenging, as therapy often involves discussing difficult emotions and experiences. Here are some strategies that can help you manage your emotions during therapy sessions:

Take deep breaths: Taking deep breaths can help you calm your body and mind when feeling overwhelmed or anxious. Take a few slow, deep breaths and focus on the sensation of the air moving in and out of your body.

Use grounding techniques: Grounding techniques can help you stay present and connected to the present moment. Some examples of grounding techniques include focusing on your senses (such as feeling your feet on the ground or breathing) or repeating a comforting phrase to yourself.

Practice self-compassion: Be gentle and compassionate with yourself when you're experiencing difficult emotions. Acknowledge your feelings and remind yourself that it's okay to feel like you do. Practice self-care activities that help you feel nurtured and supported, such as bathing or walking in nature.

Talk to your therapist: Don't be afraid to talk to your therapist about your emotions and feelings. They are trained to help you navigate difficult emotions and can provide you with support and guidance.

Use a journal: Writing down your emotions can help you process and release difficult feelings. Be honest and open, and write without worrying about grammar or spelling.

Remember that managing emotions is an ongoing process, and it's okay to feel uncomfortable or overwhelmed during therapy sessions. Using these strategies and working with your therapist can create a safe and supportive environment for exploring and processing difficult emotions.

Emotions are part of the human experience. Being upset or sad during therapy sessions is a natural part of being human. It can help to remind yourself that there's no need to try to feel less than you do because you're in counseling.

You may also want to remind yourself that whatever thoughts and emotions come up during therapy sessions are normal and that it's OK for things to feel a bit messy for a while as you work through them with your therapist.

Collaborating for a Successful Recovery Journey

The ultimate goal of recovery is to regain freedom and enjoy life again. To achieve this, you must actively participate in the recovery process.

During the recovery journey, it's important to remember that you are a team with your therapist and that your success depends on your active participation in sessions. Your therapist will provide guidance and support throughout the process, but ultimately you are responsible for changing your thinking and behavior patterns. Here are some ways to collaborate with your therapist:

Complete homework assignments: Consistent with therapeutic homework assignments can help keep you focused on goals, reduce stress, and improve your overall well-being.

Prepare for sessions: Therapy sessions can be an opportunity to work on specific issues and problems, but they can also serve as an opportunity to spend time and have fun with your therapist. If you have a topic you are working on in the session, jot down some questions or topics you want to discuss.

Ask for support: Therapy is a collaborative process; your therapist is not a mind reader. Remember that it's your responsibility to work with your therapist as a team to achieve your goals. Let them know if you're struggling or having difficulties so they can provide guidance and support.

Ask questions: Ask questions, but also be patient with your therapist. It can take your therapist a while to get to know you and clarify your goals.

Set a realistic goal: Some people find it helpful to set goals for themselves in therapy. Try setting weekly, monthly, or even annual recovery goals with your therapist so that you can track and stay on track toward achieving them.

Comply with all of your treatment recommendations: Your treatment plan is designed to help you adapt to recovery, but sometimes it can feel frustrating when you have trouble following through with the recommendations. Be patient with yourself during the process so you can reach the most positive outcome possible in therapy.

Your therapist is here to help you in any way they can, but ultimately it's your job to take ownership of your recovery. You can reach your goals if you remember that therapy is an opportunity for you and your therapist to learn skills and gain coping strategies that will empower you to recover.

CHAPTER 3

ANCHORING TO THE NOW: STOP TIME-TRAVELING AND EMBRACE THE PRESENT

This refers to staying present and focused on the current moment rather than catching up on past or future thoughts and emotions. It means embracing the present moment and fully experiencing what is happening now. It can be an effective way to reduce stress and anxiety and improve your overall sense of well-being. By focusing on the present moment and experiencing your thoughts and emotions in real-time, you can develop greater self-awareness and a deeper connection to yourself and your surroundings.

The Pitfalls of Living in the Past or Future

The past and future are not real, physical places. We use mental constructs to make sense of an infinitely complex world. They also serve to guide us in navigating a linear existence that is based on cause and effect. But while it is essential to understand the past and future, they can have very real consequences if we become overly attached to either one. And many of us do.

We all experience negative thoughts that draw us into the past and push us into the future at one time or another. This is especially true if you have been through a traumatic experience and are dealing with Complex PTSD symptoms such as emotional flashbacks, anxiety, depression, anger, guilt, and shame. These thoughts emerge in our minds unbidden. They seem to come out of nowhere for no reason at all. We try to fight them off by analyzing them and considering how we should not think this way. And we usually end up feeling worse than when the thought first came into our minds – more anxious, angry, or depressed.

The more we resist these thoughts, the stronger they get. Ironically, the more we resist them, the more they come. We become caught in a cycle of thought and emotion that can quickly take on a life of its own. And when that happens, we may succumb to these negative thoughts and start having them all the time. These thoughts can be triggered by situations that remind us of our traumatic experience or anything else that reminds us of the past or future.

Remember, the past is gone and cannot be changed. You cannot change what happened to you or what has happened to others. You can learn from it and use it to help you overcome any symptoms you are dealing with today. The future has not yet happened, and you cannot predict it with any certainty. Likewise, you cannot predict the outcome of your decisions made today. The wisest course of action is to focus on the present.

To avoid these pitfalls, it's important to cultivate mindfulness and focus on the present moment. This can help us develop greater awareness of our thoughts and emotions and learn to let go of past regrets or future worries. We can live more fulfilling and meaningful lives by staying present and engaged in the moment.

Cultivating Mindfulness for Self-Awareness

Mindfulness involves paying close attention to your thoughts, feelings, and bodily sensations and effectively coping with stressful emotions. Mindfulness helps you identify the automatic responses that can lead you into the past and future. Doing so helps you break free of the past and future tug-of-war that can trap you in self-criticism, indecision, fear, and despair.

Hypersensitivity to your surroundings is a hallmark of Complex PTSD. Many of us feel besieged by our thoughts, feelings, and bodily sensations. This hypersensitivity can lead to experiencing every little thing as a threat. We react to everyday situations with fear and anxiety when no real danger exists. It can cause us to feel on edge, unable to relax even when we are not in any physical danger. Mindfulness helps us become more aware of our thoughts, emotions, and bodily sensations without feeling overwhelmed.

It also helps you live in the present moment. Focusing on breathing makes you more attuned to your immediate surroundings and less focused on the past or future. Breathing slowly and deeply can calm your mind and alleviate stressful emotions. And by observing your thoughts and emotions, you can gain a greater awareness of yourself and your environment. This awareness is essential for recognizing triggers that may trigger a strong emotional reaction.

This practice of mindfulness is not something that comes naturally to most people. It takes time, effort, and dedication to master it. But it's well worth the trouble because as we become more attuned to our thoughts, feelings, and physical sensations, we gain better self-awareness and become less inclined to live in the past or future.

Cultivating mindfulness is a powerful way to develop self-awareness, which is recognizing and understanding our thoughts, emotions, and behaviors. Here are some ways to cultivate mindfulness for self-awareness:

Practice Meditation: Meditation is a technique that can help us focus our attention and develop greater awareness of our thoughts and emotions. By setting aside time each day to meditate, we can learn to observe our thoughts and emotions without judgment or attachment.

Pay Attention to Your Body: Our bodies provide important clues about our emotional states. We can become more aware of our emotional states by paying attention to physical sensations such as tension, pain, or discomfort.

Engage in Mindful Activities: Yoga, tai chi, or mindful breathing can help us cultivate mindfulness and self-awareness. These activities involve focusing on our breath and body sensations, which can help us become more attuned to our thoughts and emotions.

Practice Mindful Listening: Mindful listening involves paying close attention to what others say without judgment or distraction. By practicing mindful listening, we can develop greater empathy and understanding of others and cultivate greater self-awareness of our reactions and responses.

Take Mindful Breaks: Short breaks throughout the day to focus on our breath or surroundings can help us cultivate mindfulness and self-awareness. By taking a few moments to be present, we can become more aware of our thoughts and emotions and develop greater clarity and focus.

By cultivating mindfulness, we can develop greater self-awareness, which can help us better understand our thoughts, emotions, and behaviors. With this awareness, we can make more conscious choices and live more fulfilling and meaningful lives.

Techniques for Staying Present and Engaged

Staying present is the key to dealing effectively with stress. But how do we do that? One way is cultivating awareness, which can help us notice when our minds wander about the past or future. Another way is by staying engaged in the present moment. Engagement involves focusing on our breath and body sensations and keeping an open mind so we don't get obsessed with the past or worry about the future.

Here are some techniques for staying present:

Create a Balanced Schedule: Unbalanced schedules make it difficult to focus on the present moment. To stay present, we must balance work and leisure time and pay attention to our bodies, emotions, and minds.

Mindfulness Meditation: Mindfulness meditation can help us cultivate greater awareness of our thoughts and bodily sensations. By sitting in silence, we become attuned to the present moment. By observing our thoughts and emotions without judgment or attachment, we can break the hold that the past and future have on us.

Stay Engaged with Your Work: When doing something pleasurable or enjoyable, such as listening to music or reading a book, many may get lost in thinking about other activities or issues. These thoughts can distract us from being present and enjoying the activity. But if we stay engaged in the activity, we can focus on what's happening at that moment rather than worrying about something else. Engaging in a pleasurable activity can give us a sense of presence and calmness.

Grounding Techniques: Grounding techniques involve focusing on our senses to stay present in the moment. For example, focusing on the texture of a piece of fabric, the sound of a clock ticking, or the taste of a piece of fruit can help us feel more present and engaged.

Cultivating Balance: Sometimes, staying present can be challenging. Feeling stressed, anxious, or overwhelmed can cause us to feel detached from the world around us. Often we try to avoid these thoughts and emotions by being hyper-focused on our work or other pleasurable activities. But focusing on these thoughts and emotions can take us away from being present in the present moment. We must find a pathway that helps us stay grounded and in the here and now whenever possible.

Body Scan: Scanning our body from head to toe and noticing any sensations can help us become more present. This technique can help us become more aware of physical tension or discomfort and release it.

Gratitude Practice: Reflecting on what we are grateful for can help us stay present and shift our focus to positive emotions. This can help us feel more connected to the present moment and cultivate a sense of contentment and joy.

By practicing these techniques, we can become more present and engaged in the moment, which can help us better manage stress, improve our mood, and cultivate a greater sense of well-being.

Overcoming External Validation Seeking

When we feel stressed, we often seek external validation—a sign that what we feel is appropriate. Validation seeking can be very tempting when we feel stressed and worried, as it can make us feel our thoughts and feelings are justified. Seeking external validation also helps us avoid situations or people that cause us discomfort. But this approach to dealing with stress can backfire because it doesn't allow us to acknowledge that the situation or person causing our anxiety is ultimately our own.

Here are some ways to overcome external validation seeking:

Validate Your Feelings: Sometimes, when we experience negative feelings, we might not recognize them as valid signals of emotional distress and worry. To validate our feelings, we need to acknowledge them and accept them for what they are.

Stop Invalidating Yourself: When your feelings don't match how you want to feel, it's easy to invalidate yourself. This is when we talk ourselves into believing that our feelings aren't valid or shouldn't feel that way. Stop doing this! Instead, validate your feelings with self-compassion and encourage yourself to move forward by exploring the situation further or addressing the cause of your stress.

Validate the Situation: Sometimes negative situations can make us feel stressed and anxious even when no real threat exists. For example, an intense argument can make us feel insecure about a relationship in unfounded ways. Validate the situation and your feelings by seeing it as a learning opportunity.

Challenge Negative Self-Talk: Negative self-talk can contribute to external validation seeking by reinforcing our negative beliefs about ourselves. We can develop greater self-confidence and self-acceptance by challenging negative self-talk and replacing it with positive self-talk.

Set Realistic Goals: Setting goals that are achievable and aligned with our values can help us feel more self-assured and confident. We can develop greater resilience and self-efficacy by focusing on personal growth and progress rather than seeking external validation.

Focus on Internal Motivation: Rather than seeking validation from others, we can learn to be motivated by our internal desires and passions. By pursuing activities and goals that are meaningful to us, we can develop a sense of purpose and fulfillment that is not dependent on external validation.

By practicing these strategies, we can learn to rely less on external validation and develop greater self-confidence, self-acceptance, and resilience.

The Power of Embracing the Present Moment

Finding a healthy way to cope with stress is important, but we also have to use it to grow and strengthen the parts of us that are most important. Complex Post Traumatic Stress Disorder (CPTSD) is a condition where the symptoms can be debilitating and interfere with our ability to function and engage in healthy relationships. When we allow the trauma we've experienced to control and consume us, we can fall into a cycle of obsessing over past experiences, leading to more stress and trauma-related symptoms.

But by learning to embrace the present moment and accepting what is beyond our control, we can not only prevent ourselves from falling into a cycle of unhealthy coping mechanisms but also find greater meaning in our struggles.

Embracing the present moment can be a powerful tool for healing and improving their mental health. Here's how embracing the present moment can benefit individuals with C-PTSD:

Take Time for Self-Care: When we feel stressed and anxious, neglecting our personal needs is easy. Instead of attending to our emotions, we can often focus on the stresses in our lives or engage in compulsive behaviors like overeating alcohol, drug use, or other self-harming behaviors. Taking time for self-care can help us develop greater resilience and cope with stress better.

Reduces Flashbacks and Intrusive Thoughts: Individuals with C-PTSD often experience flashbacks and intrusive thoughts related to their traumatic experiences. Embracing the present moment can help individuals manage these symptoms by focusing on the present and reducing the intensity of traumatic memories.

Increases Self-Awareness: Mindfulness practices, such as focusing on the breath and bodily sensations, can help individuals with C-PTSD become more aware of their thoughts, feelings, and reactions to triggers. Individuals can better manage their symptoms and develop coping strategies by increasing self-awareness.

Enhances Emotional Regulation: Individuals with C-PTSD may experience intense emotions such as anger, fear, and sadness. Embracing the present moment can help individuals develop greater emotional regulation skills by allowing them to observe and acknowledge their emotions without being overwhelmed.

Improves Relationships: Individuals with C-PTSD may experience relationship difficulties due to symptoms such as hypervigilance, avoidance, and emotional numbing. By being present in the moment and actively listening to others, individuals can improve their communication and deepen their connections with loved ones.

Overall, embracing the present moment can be a valuable tool for individuals with C-PTSD to manage their symptoms, increase their self-awareness, and improve their quality of life. Mindfulness practices such as meditation, yoga, and breathing exercises can be useful in cultivating present-moment awareness and facilitating healing.

CHAPTER 4

IDENTITY MAKEOVER: UNCOVER THE REAL YOU BEYOND TRAUMA

After experiencing trauma, individuals may feel like their identity has been shattered or distorted. They may struggle to recognize themselves or feel disconnected from their sense of self. An Identity Makeover involves uncovering the authentic self beyond the trauma.

Trauma can profoundly impact an individual's sense of self, leading to shame, guilt, and unworthiness. Trauma can also cause individuals to adopt coping mechanisms and survival strategies that do not reflect their true selves. An Identity Makeover involves recognizing and shedding these survival strategies and exploring who the person is at their core.

Identity Makeover involves a process of self-discovery, reflection, and healing. It can involve working with a therapist to uncover the core beliefs and values that guide the individual's life. It can also involve exploring experiences, relationships, and behavior patterns to understand how they shape the person's sense of self.

An Identity Makeover is not about erasing or forgetting the trauma but acknowledging it and recognizing that it does not define the person. It is about recognizing that the person is more than their trauma and that they can shape their identity and create a life that reflects their true self.

The Struggle to Find Identity After Trauma

Many individuals struggle with their identity after experiencing trauma. Identity overhauls are one of the most commonly sought-after goals in therapy. Trauma causes individuals to feel lost and disconnected from themselves. They may struggle to recognize their sense of identity and feel like they do not know who they are. Amid trauma, they may have adopted or learned behaviors, belief systems, and ways of thinking that are inconsistent with their true selves. The struggle to find the authentic self is one of the most traumatic experiences that a person can go through.

Trauma can significantly impact a person's sense of identity, causing them to feel disconnected from themselves and struggle to find a stable sense of self. This struggle to find an identity after trauma is a common experience for many individuals who have experienced traumatic events, such as physical or emotional abuse, sexual assault, or natural disasters.

Trauma can lead to various symptoms affecting a person's sense of identity, including dissociation, depression, anxiety, and shame or guilt. These symptoms can cause individuals to feel disconnected from their bodies, emotions, and sense of self.

The struggle to find an identity after trauma often involves a process of self-discovery and exploration. This may involve working with a therapist to identify and challenge negative beliefs and behavior patterns that do not reflect the person's true self. It may also involve exploring experiences, relationships, and behavior patterns to understand how they shape the person's sense of self.

Additionally, finding identity after trauma can involve creating a sense of purpose and direction in life. This may involve pursuing meaningful activities and relationships consistent with the person's core values and beliefs.

It is important to note that finding identity after trauma is not a linear process, and there may be setbacks along the way. It requires patience, self-compassion, and a willingness to explore and understand oneself. Not only that, but it can be a challenging journey. With the right support and resources, individuals can develop a stronger and more resilient sense of identity beyond their traumatic experiences.

Ultimately, finding identity after trauma is a journey that requires patience, self-compassion, and a willingness to explore and understand oneself. Individuals must seek the support and resources to heal and build a stronger and more resilient identity. Finding a sense of identity and purpose beyond the trauma is possible with the right support.

Strategies for Personal Growth and Self-Discovery

Trauma can create tendencies and patterns that govern an individual's behaviors, thinking, and emotions. These adaptive coping mechanisms can take the form of survival strategies, which respond to a traumatic event that does not reflect the person's true self. Individuals who have experienced trauma may develop patterns involving dishonesty, secrecy, feeling disconnected from themselves and others, or aggression. These survival strategies can be difficult to change because they become ingrained in the person's thought process after experiencing trauma.

Individuals need to connect with their authentic selves to overcome these tendencies and patterns related to trauma. To do this, they need to create a sense of safety and support by seeking the resources and support they need. These resources can include therapy and developing a strong support network.

One way for individuals to get in touch with their authentic selves is through self-discovery, which involves exploring thoughts, feelings, experiences, relationships, and patterns of behavior that reflect who they are at their core. Individuals need to explore these things in a safe space where they feel supported and guided by those around them. This can be done through therapy or with the help of trusted family members or friends.

Another way for individuals to get in touch with their authentic selves is through personal growth strategies. These ways of responding to a traumatic event are consistent with the individual's core values, beliefs, and true self. It involves breaking old habits and patterns to develop new ways of responding to healthier situations that reflect the person's true self.

Some effective personal growth and self-discovery strategies include:

Journaling: Writing down your thoughts and feelings can help you gain clarity and insight into yourself. It can also help you identify patterns in your behavior and thought processes.

Mindfulness: Practicing mindfulness can help you develop an awareness of your thoughts, emotions, and bodily sensations in the present moment. This can help you identify and regulate your emotional responses and make more conscious choices.

Therapy: Working with a therapist can provide a safe and supportive environment to explore your thoughts, feelings, and behaviors. It can also help you identify and challenge negative beliefs and behavior patterns that may hold you back.

Self-care: Practicing self-care can help you prioritize your physical, emotional, and mental health. This can include activities like exercise, meditation, time in nature, or engaging in hobbies that bring you joy.

Seeking new experiences: Trying new things can help you expand your perspective and challenge your comfort zone. This can include traveling to new places, taking up a hobby, or meeting new people.

Remember, personal growth and self-discovery are ongoing processes that require patience, self-compassion, and a willingness to be vulnerable. With time and effort, these strategies can help you better understand yourself and cultivate a more fulfilling and meaningful life.

Building Resilience for a Stronger Sense of Self

Resilience is the ability to bounce back from difficult situations and cope with stress and adversity. Building resilience can help you develop a stronger sense of self, increase your ability to handle challenges, and improve your overall well-being.

When an individual experiences a traumatic event, it can cause them to question their true self. This can seem like a chance for growth and development, but it can also amplify existing trauma-related tendencies and patterns. These tendencies and patterns can be overwhelming and lead to hopelessness or helplessness. It is common for individuals who have experienced trauma to lose hope or become overwhelmed with negative emotions. This often leaves them questioning whether the healing process after trauma is worthwhile or meaningful.

However, there are ways in which individuals can build resilience for a stronger sense of identity that is worth exploring. This involves creating new ways of interacting with the world that allow them to become more authentic and reflective of their true selves. Some strategies for building resilience include:

Self-compassion: Self-compassion involves being kind and understanding towards yourself when you make mistakes or encounter stressful situations. It involves recognizing that you are not alone and having supportive people.

Practice self-care: Taking care of your physical, emotional, and mental health can help you cope with stress and adversity. This can include exercise, healthy eating, getting enough sleep, and engaging in activities that bring you joy.

Cultivate supportive relationships: A strong support system can give you a sense of belonging and help you cope with difficult situations. This can include friends, family members, or support groups.

Develop problem-solving skills: Learning to identify problems and develop effective solutions can help you feel more in control and capable of handling difficult situations.

Practice mindfulness: Practicing mindfulness can help you develop an awareness of your thoughts, emotions, and bodily sensations in the present moment. This can help you regulate your emotional responses and make more conscious choices.

Reframe negative thinking: Learning to challenge and reframe negative thoughts can help you develop a more positive outlook and increase your resilience.

Build on past successes: Reflecting on past successes and achievements can help you build confidence and resilience.

Remember, building resilience is an ongoing process that requires time, effort, and a willingness to learn and grow. By practicing these strategies, you can develop a stronger sense of self and increase your ability to cope with stress and adversity.

Redefining Your Values and Beliefs

When an individual experiences a traumatic event, it can cause them to question their values and beliefs. This can seem like a chance for growth, but it can also amplify negative patterns of behavior and thought processes. These overwhelming patterns can lead to a sense of hopelessness or helplessness.

It is common for individuals who have experienced trauma to become preoccupied with self-doubt and negative thoughts about the world around them. These negative thoughts can make it more difficult for them to enjoy life or feel optimistic about the future. This often leaves them questioning whether they can hold onto their values and beliefs in adversity.

However, there are ways in which individuals can redefine their values and beliefs for a sense of hope and optimism that are worth exploring. This involves creating new ways of interacting with the world that allow them to become more authentic and reflective of their true selves. Some strategies for redefining your values and beliefs include:

Identify personal strengths and resources: Identifying your strengths and resources can help you get through difficult situations more effectively. It can also help you take control of your life and become more resilient.

Develop self-determined life goals: Setting goals for yourself that you feel truly can help you take control of your life and make it more meaningful.

Befriend others with similar challenges: People with similar values or beliefs can benefit your well-being. This can allow you access to a supportive community of positive people who can encourage each other to keep going when things are difficult.

Reflect on your current values and beliefs: Consider what values and beliefs are important to you. Consider what motivates you and gives your life meaning.

Identify any values or beliefs that no longer serve you: Trauma can sometimes leave us holding onto beliefs and values that no longer serve us. Identify any values or beliefs that may be holding you back or causing you distress.

Clarify your values: Identify the values that are most important to you, such as compassion, honesty, or creativity. Clarifying your values can help you stay focused on what truly matters to you and guide your decision-making.

Challenge your limiting beliefs: Identify any beliefs holding you back and challenge them. Ask yourself if there is evidence to support these beliefs or if they are based on assumptions or negative self-talk.

Explore new beliefs and values: Consider exploring new beliefs and values that align with who you are now and what you want to achieve. This can include finding new hobbies, exploring spirituality, or learning about different cultures and perspectives.

Remember, redefining your values and beliefs is a personal process that takes time and self-reflection. Be patient with yourself and celebrate your progress along the way.

Embracing the Journey of Self-Exploration

The journey of healing from trauma is a struggle that requires time, patience, support, and a willingness to learn and grow. It can be an intimidating process without any clear indicators of progress or success. This can leave you feeling stuck and unable to move forward. However, there are certain strategies that you can use to keep yourself moving forward and take charge of your recovery.

One way you can embrace your journey of self-exploration is by thinking about the process as a series of challenges that have helped you learn and grow. Rather than feeling defeated by the challenges, look at them as opportunities for growth. Identify how you feel when facing challenges and reflect on what has helped you overcome them in the past. This can be a good way to become more mindful of how your thoughts and emotions affect your behavior.

Another way to embrace your journey is by using positive self-talk. When you are struggling to move forward, take a moment to reflect on how you are feeling. Be honest about the difficulty and recognize how far you have come. Then remind yourself that all emotions and challenges will pass given enough time and support. Remember that you can pull through this given the right tools and resources.

For many people who have experienced trauma, self-exploration can feel debilitating without any clear sign of progress or success. However, embracing your journey can help create a balanced perspective around your recovery process. It can motivate and encourage you to continue moving forward when nothing seems to be working.

People who have experienced trauma sometimes find it hard to move forward. They feel trapped within themselves. They may find themselves focusing on the negative, which can lead them to feel anxious and anxious about the future. Most of all, they may feel scared of what lies ahead and what they will be left with when helping has ended.

Embracing the journey of self-exploration can be a powerful way to heal from trauma and rediscover your sense of self. Here are some strategies for embracing this journey:

Be open to what you are learning about yourself: Self-exploration can be a powerful way to learn about yourself. Rather than feeling overwhelmed by all that you have experienced, learn from it and embrace the lessons that you have learned. All of your experiences—both positive and negative—contain valuable insights into who you are.

Take time to reflect: Another way to embrace your journey is by reflecting on who you are now. Take a journal, go on long walks in nature, or meditate to help find insights into how your mind works and how you relate to the world around you.

Explore new possibilities: Take time to explore new possibilities for yourself and what you want out of life. Consider what activities help you feel fulfilled and how to incorporate more of these into your daily routine.

Remember, self-exploration is a process that does not work for everyone. It can be hard for some people to embrace this journey, especially if they feel defensive, guarded, or angry. If self-exploration is triggering or causing you distress, consider getting professional help to guide you through this process in a safe and supportive way.

CHAPTER 5

QUIT THE BLAME GAME: OWN YOUR HEALING AND THRIVE

This means taking responsibility for your healing journey instead of blaming others for your struggles. It involves acknowledging that while trauma and difficult experiences can profoundly impact your life, it is ultimately up to you to take control of your healing and move forward.

Blaming others is a self-fulfilling prophecy of doom. This approach makes you feel like you can never move on and will be stuck in the trauma and difficult experiences cycle. It takes away your hope, and it takes away your power.

Instead, look at all the circumstances in your life that have caused you pain but have allowed you to grow and mature, as well as new lessons that have come out of that pain. Remember that if it weren't for difficult experiences, we would stagnate as human beings. This means taking ownership of the painful circumstances in your life to learn more about yourself and how to heal from them.

The Trap of Blaming Others

You may use the blame game as a defense mechanism to avoid taking responsibility for your healing. You may blame external factors or people for all your pain and disappointment. While it is natural to look at others and wonder why they don't behave the way we want them to, it can be an avoidance strategy that keeps you in your struggle instead of out of it. Ultimately, playing the blame game can only reinforce feelings of hurt, anger, betrayal, and fear or anxiety.

While it is always important to look at ways that families of origin can contribute to our unhelpful beliefs and perceptions after trauma, it is crucial not to lose sight of yourself as well. Developing a healthy relationship with yourself will not only be more helpful for overcoming your struggles, but it will also allow you to be compassionate and have compassion for others. When we can care for ourselves, it enables us to be the kind of person that others want to be around.

Blaming others is a common trap when struggling with trauma or difficult experiences. It can feel easier to point the finger at someone else for our problems rather than take responsibility for our healing. However, blaming others can be damaging and prevent you from moving forward in your healing journey.

Here are some reasons why blaming others can be harmful:

It gives away your power: When you blame others for your problems, you give it to someone else. This can leave you feeling helpless and stuck.

It perpetuates negative emotions: Blaming others can keep you in negative emotions like anger, resentment, and bitterness. These emotions can be harmful to your mental and physical health.

It can damage relationships: Blaming others can strain relationships and make it difficult to repair trust and connection.

It doesn't lead to resolution: Blaming others does not lead to resolution or healing. It only perpetuates negative emotions and can make it harder to move forward.

Instead of blaming others, taking responsibility for your healing journey is important. This involves acknowledging the impact of trauma or difficult experiences on your life and recognizing that you can make positive changes. You can move towards a more positive and fulfilling future by taking ownership of your healing journey and focusing on positive actions.

Taking Responsibility for Your Healing Journey

Taking responsibility for your healing journey means recognizing your positive qualities and acknowledging which things are out of your control. It involves taking small steps each day to build confidence and self-love. You can heal wounds, build resilience, and move towards a brighter future by embracing your healing with renewed hope and optimism.

Taking responsibility means acknowledging that difficult experiences, such as trauma and loss, can profoundly impact our lives, but they do not completely control us. Realizing that we have the power to make choices in our lives is an important part of taking responsibility for our recovery from trauma. This means acknowledging your strengths, abilities, and accomplishments while also respecting the limits you may have after difficult experiences.

This may include looking at how others have contributed to your struggle, but it is equally important to consider what you can do for yourself. This can involve finding a support network of friends and loved ones who will be there for you and encouraging healthy habits that promote a sense of calm and balance. It can also involve being honest about your struggles and taking positive actions daily to build confidence, self-love, and connection.

Taking responsibility for your healing journey will build resilience and help you feel more confident. Learning to take responsibility for your healing journey after difficult experiences takes practice. However, it can become easier once you commit to doing so.

Here are some ways that you can take responsibility for your healing journey:

Admit your struggle: Begin by acknowledging the impact trauma or difficult experiences have had on your life. It is also important to acknowledge that it is okay for you to be struggling, and it is okay if you feel overwhelmed. This does not make you a bad person or weak. It only shows that recovery from trauma is hard work.

Identify a support network of friends and loved ones: When it comes to healing after trauma, having people in your life who support recovery and care about how you are doing can be very helpful. Knowing that you have people who care about your well-being can tremendously boost your healing process.

Set small goals: Some ways to take responsibility for your healing journey include identifying daily small and short-term goals. For example, you can use the SMART acronym (Specific, Measurable, Attainable, Realistic, and Time-bound) to help you align your healing with success. As a therapeutic tool, it is important to define what you want from your life. This can include identifying long-term and short-term goals so that you know where to focus on leading a more fulfilling life after trauma or difficult experiences.

Sometimes identifying these goals will be easier with the help of a therapist, partner, friend, or family member. Just because you work to take responsibility for your healing journey doesn't mean you have to do everything alone. Having a support network of people who care about your recovery can make it easier to identify small and short-term goals for each day.

Taking daily steps towards a more fulfilling life is an important part of taking responsibility for your healing journey. This can include setting up reminders on your phone, adding healthy habits into your daily routine, and practicing self-care. While acknowledging the importance of self-care, it is equally important to take care of yourself by setting small daily goals. This can include identifying your priorities and making small steps to help you get closer to achieving them.

Dealing with trauma: When it comes to dealing with trauma and difficult experiences, there are many things that you can do on your own, including talking about how you are feeling. By discussing what happened in a calm, non-judgmental way, it may become easier to process the incident and start healing from the traumatic experience.

Other methods you can use on your own include exercising, engaging in self-care practices such as mindfulness, spending time with friends and loved ones, and creating a mood journal.

Talking to a professional, such as a therapist, social worker, or spiritual leader, can also be helpful when taking responsibility for your healing journey after trauma. This could be especially true if the trauma occurred within the context of abuse or sexual assault.

When talking to someone about the pain of trauma, it is often helpful to go at your own pace. When talking about a traumatic experience for the first time, it may help to practice identifying your feelings without trying to analyze what happened in detail. Instead, try expressing your feelings non-judgmentally and just talking about what you are experiencing.

As you work on taking responsibility for your healing journey after trauma, it is important to remember that no one can make your healing go faster. It is almost impossible for anyone to do this. Once you begin to work on your healing process, allowing yourself time and space is important.

This can include doing things differently than before or paying attention to how you feel physically and emotionally at different times throughout the day. This can involve writing in a mood diary about how you feel so that you can track your moods, thoughts, and behaviors.

An important part of taking responsibility for your healing journey after trauma is learning to recognize when to take steps toward self-care and when it is okay to give yourself a break. When you are working on your healing process, it can help to talk with friends, loved ones, or professional therapists so that they can provide support. Knowing that you have people who care about your well-being and want to see you heal can be very reassuring.

Shifting Focus to Personal Growth and Accountability

Shifting focus from blame and control to personal growth and accountability is key to resilience.

Taking responsibility for your healing journey is an important part of individual growth after difficult experiences or trauma. This includes taking steps to help others recover from similar experiences, learning to be accountable for yourself in stressful situations, and being able to take responsibility for your happiness.

Taking action toward personal growth can be one of the most important parts of taking responsibility for your healing journey after trauma or difficult experiences. To become an agent of positive change regarding these topics, it is important first to understand what you have been through, why you have gone through these events and the impact it had on you and others.

Exploring events in your life can also be a part of taking responsibility for your healing journey. After difficult experiences, it is important to take the time to understand what has happened and why it has happened. To take personal responsibility for your healing journey, you must acknowledge the impact of difficult experiences on your life.

Taking personal responsibility after reading or watching stories triggered by traumatic or difficult experiences can also help you understand how these events impact others in similar situations. These stories can be helpful in that they allow you to gain knowledge, understanding, and perspective about traumatic or difficult experiences.

As you are working on your healing process, it is important to acknowledge the impact of difficult experiences on yourself and others. By taking this approach to your healing journey, you can be an agent of growth and change.

Some of the most important steps toward growth and change include learning to accept how things have happened and what has occurred. This can include learning not to blame others for how these events have been processed.

Taking more responsibility for your healing journey can also involve taking time to recognize the progress that you have made. This is important because it allows you to acknowledge the work that you have done to deal with the impact of difficult experiences or trauma.

These steps can be some of the most powerful ways for you to move forward and grow as an individual healthily.

Letting Go of Resentment and Anger

Letting go of resentment and anger is an important part of taking responsibility for your healing journey after trauma or difficult experiences.

Resentment and anger are common emotions that can arise after trauma or difficult experiences. It is common for you to resent someone who hurt you or failed to protect you from harm. These feelings might also arise towards others who were present when the event occurred but could not help, especially when the traumatic experience involved abuse.

Resentment may also be aimed at those directly involved in the traumatic experience because they perpetrated it, such as sexual assault or physical abuse.

The emotions of resentment and anger can be powerful and can often consume you; this is why it is so important to let them go to move forward and take steps toward personal growth.

To let go of feelings of resentment, you, first of all, need to learn how they are impacting your life. You must understand how these feelings can control your thoughts, emotions, and behaviors.

You must also acknowledge the role that resentment plays in your life. For example, do these feelings manifest themselves in a different way each day? When this occurs, it may help to practice breathing or relaxation techniques when you notice these more intense feelings of resentment arise.

Resentment is often associated with negative thoughts and emotions that can be self-sustaining and difficult to release. This is why learning to change your resentment is important to move forward on your healing journey.

For example, it may help if you reframe your thoughts by trying to remember the positive aspects of relationships with certain people instead of focusing solely on the negative aspects. Reframing negative thoughts may also be achieved by making a conscious effort to spend less time thinking about these people or events from the past, which will ultimately help reduce the emotional impact they have on you.

But, letting go of resentment involves learning to change your thoughts and feelings about certain events and people that can trigger resentment.

It can also be helpful to use writing or drawing to express and release these feelings since they may be difficult to communicate verbally. A verbal outlet can help you move on from these memories and experiences.

This kind of expression can help you focus on the future instead of dwelling on the past because it allows you to release this negativity healthily. It would help if you spent time thinking about your future so that it becomes part of your positive thoughts.

These kinds of techniques can be beneficial to you in taking steps toward your healing journey.

Embracing Empowerment in Recovery

Empowerment is important to taking responsibility for your healing journey after trauma or difficult experiences. For you to heal healthily, it is often helpful for you to embrace and move forward with empowerment.

Embracing empowerment can include making conscious choices about what you want from life and giving yourself the power to achieve these goals by taking daily steps toward your overall health and well-being.

Embracing empowerment in recovery means taking an active role in your healing journey and reclaiming your power. It involves shifting your focus from what has happened to you in the past to what you can do now to create a better future for yourself. Empowerment in recovery involves recognizing that you have the power to make choices, set boundaries, and take action to create positive change in your life.

Here are some ways to embrace empowerment in your recovery:

Take ownership of your healing journey: Recognize that you are in charge of your healing journey and that you can make choices that will benefit your recovery.

Set boundaries: Boundaries are important in recovery because they help protect you from harmful situations and relationships. Setting boundaries involves saying no to things, not in your best interest and prioritizing your well-being.

Focus on your strengths: Getting caught up in what you lack or are struggling with is easy. Instead, focus on your strengths and the positive qualities you possess. This can help to boost your confidence and self-esteem.

Practice self-care: Self-care is an important part of recovery. Taking care of your physical, emotional, and mental health can help you to feel more empowered and in control of your life.

Surround yourself with positive influences: Surround yourself with people who support and encourage you in your recovery. This can include friends, family, support groups, or a therapist.

Learn new skills: Learning new skills can help you build confidence and self-esteem. This can include anything from taking a class to learning a new hobby or practicing a new mindfulness technique.

By embracing empowerment in your recovery, you can create a positive and fulfilling future for yourself. It involves recognizing your strength and resilience and building on those qualities to create a better life for yourself.

CHAPTER 6

NO ≠ ABANDONMENT: DECODE REJECTION AND KEEP CALM

The fear of rejection is a common experience for many people, especially those who have experienced trauma or difficult life experiences. It can be challenging to navigate feelings of rejection and understand that being told "no" does not necessarily mean abandonment or a reflection of your worth. Complex Post Traumatic Stress Disorder (C-PTSD) often includes heightened sensitivity to rejection, which can exacerbate symptoms associated with abandonment. If you struggle with rejection, it is important to recognize potential ways your thought process is negatively impacting your life.

Understanding the Fear of Abandonment in c-PTSD

When you have experienced abandonment in the past, the fear of abandonment can become ingrained in your life. You may have an irrational belief that you will suffer dire consequences if rejected or abandoned. You may believe that your ability to function as a person will be threatened. This is not true. The truth is that being told "no" or rejected by someone does not mean you are worthless. It does not mean that you will have no friends. It does not mean that you won't find love again. The fear of abandonment is irrational; therefore, it is important to try and combat it with rational understanding and coping tools for rejection-based setbacks in life.

The fear of abandonment is a common symptom experienced by individuals with complex post-traumatic stress disorder (C-PTSD). This fear is rooted in your experiences of being abandoned, neglected, or rejected by important people. For someone with C-PTSD, being told "no," or being rejected by a loved one or potential partner can be painful and distressing. To the uninitiated, it might seem like those with C-PTSD's reaction to rejection is overblown or irrational. However, if you understand the fear of abandonment and how it works in C-PTSD individuals, you will be better equipped to cope successfully. If you are rocking with c-PTSD, you have experienced some trauma that has been extremely disruptive and painful at some point in your life. This pain and suffering have been so deep that it has imprinted on your psyche, making you hyper-vigilant about potential threats and danger. In this way, the fear of abandonment is, in many ways, an adaptive response. This way of thinking led you to survive a painful situation in the past. But it also keeps you from fully enjoying life now because you constantly fear rejection or abandonment by someone important to you.

This fear can manifest in various ways, such as becoming overly dependent on others, being overly jealous or possessive in relationships, or avoiding close relationships altogether. The fear of abandonment can also lead to feelings of anxiety, depression, and low self-esteem.

It is important to note that the fear of abandonment is not a sign of weakness or character flaw but rather a natural response to past trauma. Recognizing and acknowledging this fear is an important step toward healing and recovery.

Therapy can effectively address the fear of abandonment and develop coping skills to manage it. It is also important to work on building a strong support system of trusted individuals who can provide reassurance and stability in times of stress or uncertainty.

Tools for Recognizing and Managing Emotional Responses

When you experience rejection, there are steps you can take to help yourself deal with the experience. First, remember that not all rejections are personal and are often beyond your control. Rejections can happen at work while trying to make new friends or in romantic situations. Realizing that some rejections aren't personal is important because when we feel rejected, we often interpret it as a reflection of who we are. But if we remember that some rejections have nothing to do with us as individuals, it is easier to manage the emotional impact of rejection.

Effective coping skills for dealing with rejection are essential for anyone who has experienced trauma or difficulty. The following steps can help you manage your emotional response to rejection:

1. Recognize That Rejection Does Not Mean you are Unlovable

Your experiences in life have shaped you into a unique individual. Rejections do not reflect who you are as a person. No one is perfect, and everyone makes mistakes.

2. Recognize the Times When Rejection Is Personal

Rejections are very personal, but not always. Sometimes rejections can happen at work, in social situations, or from people, we thought were close to us. It is important to evaluate whether the rejection is personal and whether it indicates that someone does not like you or thinks your behavior has been inappropriate or unacceptable in some way.

3. Do Not Blame Yourself.

Take a moment to evaluate what you have done in the situation and what you will do differently in the future to prevent similar circumstances. Whatever mistakes have been made, it is important not to blame yourself.

4. Try and Understand the Rejection

Sometimes people reject you because they have other reasons or personal issues that are causing them to act in a way that is hurtful or harmful to you. It is important to try and understand this perspective rather than dwell on your feelings about rejection.

5. Use it as an Opportunity for Personal Growth

We all make mistakes in life, but this does not mean we cannot learn from them and become better human beings. Rejection can be a good learning experience, especially if it is your fault and not someone else's. This opportunity can help you become a better person who can identify and correct mistakes in the future.

6. Understand Rejection as an Inevitable Part of Life

Rejections happen to all of us, and we can do nothing about it. However, now, you have control over how you respond and choose to act in the future. This control is something that we should all strive for.

Developing Healthier Interpretations of Rejection

It is important to understand why someone rejects you. This can help you differentiate between personal rejection and rejection that has nothing to do with you as an individual. It is also important to analyze your behavior and take responsibility for your decisions about how people treat you.

When we allow ourselves to believe that our experiences are personally relevant, we will experience more emotional pain due to rejection by others. If we feel like something someone says or does means they do not like or value us, it can cause emotional damage and make us feel bad about ourselves.

Although society can place a great deal of emphasis on how a person's appearance impacts their value to us, the truth is that we are all beautiful and lovable no matter what we look like. We all have the same basic needs for love and acceptance, which should be enough to lift our spirits.

The truth is that rejection happens all the time in life. Many people will experience rejection without realizing that this is what has happened. This can cause them to become more insecure during certain situations and lead them to make decisions that will create more pain in their lives later on. Being aware of these facts about rejection can help us break free from the damaging cycle of emotional pain caused by our interpretations of rejections.

Developing healthier interpretations of rejection involves challenging negative thoughts and beliefs that may fuel our fear of abandonment. Here are some strategies for doing so:

Challenge your assumptions: When you feel rejected, it is important to challenge your assumptions about the situation. Ask yourself, "What evidence do I have that supports my belief that I am being abandoned?" and "What evidence contradicts my belief?"

Reframe rejection as redirection: Instead of seeing rejection as a reflection of your worth, try to see it as a redirection towards something better suited for you. This can help you see rejection as an opportunity rather than a failure.

Practice self-compassion: Be kind and compassionate towards yourself when you experience rejection. Acknowledge your pain and remind yourself that it is a natural human emotion.

Seek support: Reach out to friends, family, or a therapist when you feel rejected. A supportive network can help you reframe rejection healthily and feel less alone in your experience.

By challenging negative thoughts and beliefs about rejection, reframing rejection as redirection, practicing self-compassion, and seeking support, we can develop healthier interpretations of rejection and reduce the impact of our fear of abandonment.

Building Self-Awareness and Emotional Regulation

Self-awareness and emotional regulation are key skills that can help us manage our fear of abandonment more effectively. By developing both of these skills, we can learn to understand the impact of rejection in the past on our emotions and behaviors and how these experiences could potentially affect the rest of our lives.

To become more self-aware of our past experiences with rejection, we must take the time to reflect on how these experiences have affected us. This self-reflection can help us understand how different situations have impacted us and avoid making the same mistakes in our current relationships.

Emotional regulation is another skill we can gain as we learn to manage our emotions better in different social situations. This skill is vital for controlling our fears of abandonment as we make new friends, go on dates, or interact with people.

The first step to building emotional regulation is learning to identify the emotions that arise when you experience rejection and labeling these feelings in an observable way. When we pay attention to our emotions, ignoring them becomes much more difficult, and they tend to subside more quickly.

To build emotional regulation, we can practice new behaviors and increase the number of situations in which we can handle rejection appropriately.

Here are some ways that you can become more self-aware and develop emotional regulation skills:

Identify your emotions: Pay attention to the feelings that arise when something happens that seems like it might be a rejection. Simply observing these feelings will help you learn how they feel and how they usually respond to certain situations. This awareness can allow you to react differently in the future in these situations so that you are not as easily hurt by them.

Name your emotions: This step can also be done publicly or externally. If you feel rejected by someone, say, "I feel hurt right now." If you are angry, shout, "I'm angry!" If you are afraid, say "I'm afraid" instead. Make this part of your conversations with others to make the feelings more obvious.

Utilize self-motivation: When we fear something and want to avoid it, we tend not to do anything about it. As a result of this fear and its inherent procrastination, we often repeatedly fall into the same traps. To become emotionally regulated, we must use self-motivation to take action and overcome the fear of rejection.

Exercise emotional regulation: It can be difficult to feel emotionally regulated when we experience rejection. We may want to avoid feeling these emotions but developing emotional regulation skills will help us learn how to handle them healthily.

Practice assertiveness: When we find ourselves in situations that seem like they might be a rejection, we often feel embarrassed and do not know what to say or do. You can begin improving at taking action by doing assertiveness training with a therapist or coach. They can help you learn how to express your feelings healthily so that you will be less afraid of rejection by others.

Take responsibility: Stop blaming others for your feelings of rejection and start taking responsibility for them yourself. By taking responsibility for your feelings, you will be better able to deal with the situations that trigger them in the future.

Critical self-reflection: It is important to reflect on the past and see how our experiences with rejection have shaped us into the people we are today. Developing self-awareness and emotional regulation can help us learn more about these experiences and avoid making the same mistakes in the future.

Fostering Secure and Fulfilling Relationships

There are many reasons we might fear abandonment, and learning to manage the fear of abandonment can help us develop healthier relationships and become more attractive to others. The fear of abandonment is an important part of our personality, but it can also cause us to react to others in unhealthy and avoidant ways.

The fear of rejection can lead us to act avoidant when interacting with others, as we believe they will abandon us or treat us poorly if things do not go well. When we experience rejection, this behavior can most likely be attributed to poor self-esteem or self-confidence. Developing healthy self-worth and being more assertive in our interactions with others are important to build the security we desperately want and need.

The fear of rejection can also cause us to become too dependent on others. This is especially true for those who are in a relationship and anticipate being left by their partners. Dependent people tend to avoid taking risks in their relationships and relationships overall, which can ultimately lead to the demise of these important relationships.

To overcome these fears, it is extremely important that we first learn how to be assertive instead of avoidant and begin building secure and fulfilling relationships with others.

To build secure relationships, we must understand ourselves better and learn to accept our flaws while embracing our strengths. We need to know that we are worthy of love, respect, and attention from others and that independence and autonomy are okay.

Fostering secure and fulfilling relationships is essential to healing from complex PTSD. Trauma can disrupt our ability to trust and connect with others, making it challenging to form healthy relationships. Here are some strategies for fostering secure and fulfilling relationships:

Practice vulnerability: It can be scary to open up and share your feelings with others, especially if you have experienced trauma. However, being vulnerable and sharing your authentic self with others can help build trust and deepen connections.

Communicate effectively: Effective communication is essential for building healthy relationships. This includes being able to express your needs and boundaries, as well as being able to listen and respond to others in a non-judgmental way.

Set healthy boundaries: Healthy boundaries are important to any relationship. This involves being clear about your needs and limits and communicating them to others in a respectful way.

Practice empathy: Empathy is the ability to understand and share the feelings of others. It can help build connections and strengthen relationships by showing others that you care and are willing to listen and support them.

Seek professional help if needed: If you struggle with building and maintaining healthy relationships, seeking professional help can be beneficial. A therapist can provide support and guidance as you work on developing healthier relationship patterns.

By practicing these strategies, you can build secure and fulfilling relationships supporting your healing journey.

CHAPTER 7

SENSITIVITY TAKEDOWN: STAY COOL IN THE HEAT OF SOCIAL ENCOUNTERS

This refers to the idea of managing one's sensitivity in social situations. It involves learning how to stay calm and composed when faced with challenging social encounters that may trigger feelings of anxiety or overwhelm. This could be particularly relevant for individuals who struggle with social anxiety or have experienced trauma that has made them more sensitive to social situations. Sensitivity takedown aims to develop effective coping strategies allowing individuals to navigate social situations more easily and confidently.

Interpersonal Hypersensitivity and c-PTSD

Interpersonal hypersensitivity refers to a tendency to be hyper-sensitive or overactive to the perceived intentions of others. This is frequently seen in individuals who have developed c-PTSD and is commonly manifested in misinterpretations of social situations, hostile responses to people's actions, and a tendency towards anger or aggressive behavior in response to interpersonal stressors. Individuals who experience symptoms of interpersonal hypersensitivity cannot easily read between the lines when interpreting the motivations and intentions of others. They tend not to be able to see things from another's perspective or acknowledge that others may have different expectations or values than they do. As such, they may perceive others as having negative intentions toward them when expressing their needs or wishes. Individuals with interpersonal hypersensitivity often struggle to maintain stable and healthy interpersonal relationships, as they regularly perceive others as hostile or cruel towards them. This leads individuals with c-PTSD to feel misunderstood, isolated, and rejected by others.

Individuals with c-PTSD may have developed this hypersensitivity as a coping mechanism to survive past traumatic experiences, such as emotional, physical, or sexual abuse. The trauma may have led to a heightened sensitivity to interpersonal cues as a means of self-preservation. However, this hypersensitivity can cause distress and interfere with daily functioning.

Some common signs of interpersonal hypersensitivity in c-PTSD include:

- Overreacting to perceived social slights or rejection
- Avoiding social situations or withdrawing from relationships
- Feeling chronically insecure or inadequate in social situations
- Difficulty setting boundaries or saying no
- Feeling like others are always judging or criticizing them

Individuals with c-PTSD need to recognize these patterns and work towards developing healthier coping strategies to manage their interpersonal hypersensitivity. This may involve therapy, mindfulness practices, and developing self-compassion and self-esteem.

Coping Strategies for Managing Emotional Reactions

One way to manage hypersensitivity is through developing effective coping strategies that allow individuals to be more resilient and less reactive to the emotional stressors they are faced with. Ineffective coping strategies may lead to feelings of exhaustion, despair, fear, and frustration in response to interpersonal stressors. This is a common problem for individuals who have developed c-PTSD and hypersensitivity. Individuals may feel overwhelmed by their emotions or experience dark thoughts about the future due to anxiety and stress about what others think or expect of them. An important step towards managing interpersonal hypersensitivity is to learn to focus one's energy on understanding and addressing the underlying emotional needs in a given situation. Then, with this insight, individuals can develop more effective methods of communication or coping strategies to address these needs.

Further, identifying and processing strong emotions may allow individuals with c-PTSD to feel more self-assured in social situations and increase their capacity for healthy interpersonal relationships. By avoiding or ignoring all of their emotions, individuals may feel vulnerable, anxious, or lost when faced with interpersonal stressors. Identifying and processing emotions effectively is an important step toward coping with them when they arise.

Navigating Social Situations With Confidence

Learning to navigate social situations effectively with confidence may be challenging for individuals with hypersensitivity and c-PTSD. Many people with PTSD have experienced extensive trauma, which can leave them feeling insecure and overwhelmed when they think of approaching new social situations. It is important for individuals who struggle with hypersensitivity to develop effective strategies for managing the stressors associated with their hypersensitivity. This includes learning to regulate themselves, including breathing exercises, meditation or mindfulness practices, or other relaxation strategies. One way to practice self-regulation is by establishing healthy boundaries and practicing assertive communication. This allows individuals to set clear expectations of interactions and establish agreeable limits while maintaining appropriate contact with others.

When practicing assertive communication, individuals should explain what they expect from others while being honest and direct. This can be accomplished by asking someone if they have time to meet or if texting them later is okay. However, setting boundaries is much more difficult for some people than others, as this requires self-awareness and mindfulness skills. Sometimes learning how to navigate social situations by understanding how people perceive your hypersensitivity can help you develop more effective coping strategies for managing it healthily.

There are also some other healthy ways to cope with hypersensitivity. Simple activities, like exercising and spending time alone, may help individuals relax and reflect on their day. Additionally, individuals can learn to care for themselves through regular exercise, healthy eating, and getting enough sleep. This can make them feel more confident about their appearance in social settings. Being assertive about your needs and learning to identify your feelings are important for individuals who struggle with c-PTSD. However, it is important not to let these coping strategies become an excuse for one's hypersensitivity or interpersonal stressors. No matter how challenging, developing healthy relationships with others is an important coping skill for any individual.

Strengthening Emotional Boundaries

Individuals with c-PTSD may need to strengthen their emotional boundaries to cope with hypersensitivity and the associated stress. Emotional boundaries are important for establishing a sense of space between an individual and others, setting healthy boundaries for interpersonal relationships, and recognizing when others take advantage of their kindness or compassion. Healthy relationships involve frequent emotional exchanges, but these give-and-take interactions should be balanced.

The first step in strengthening emotional boundaries is to learn how to separate your thoughts from those of others. As described above, people who experience c-PTSD may have developed hypersensitivity as a survival skill activated in stressful situations. Sometimes this makes individuals feel responsible for what others think or feel about them. However, this skill can be learned through mindfulness practices or therapy. It can help individuals establish a sense of self-confidence and self-worth as individuals.

Another way to strengthen emotional boundaries is by setting clear expectations for the relationships you will engage in. Being assertive about what you expect from others lets you clearly state your needs and limits during social interactions. This is an important step towards developing healthy interpersonal relationships and feeling confident in those relationships. If someone is taking advantage of you or not sticking to the boundaries you have laid out, it becomes much easier to recognize these situations as harmful interactions.

Another way to strengthen emotional boundaries is to develop appropriate expectations for emotions you might experience in a given situation (positive or negative). It can be helpful to know that all emotions are normal and acceptable, and a healthy boundary will involve recognizing and processing these feelings while they are occurring. Individuals with c-PTSD may have difficulty distinguishing between their thoughts and those of others, making it difficult to process unavoidable social stressors without making themselves sick or overreacting. Learning how to recognize the healthy emotions of others in certain situations can help individuals respond more healthily when faced with interpersonal stressors.

Another important step in strengthening emotional boundaries is learning to process emotions appropriately. People with c-PTSD may have difficulty regulating everyday emotions such as frustration or anger, especially when it involves interpersonal interactions with others. This can lead to hypersensitivity and inappropriate reactions when someone does not behave as forecasted by the person with c-PTSD. Learning how to respond to social stressors healthily can help individuals with hypersensitivity cope with their impairments.

It is important for individuals who struggle with hypersensitivity to understand that their feelings are not wrong or invalid but simply a normal part of human interaction. Even if not warranted, identifying anger or frustration can help individuals recognize and process their emotional responses healthily. This can be a step towards developing healthy emotional boundaries amid interpersonal situations.

Building a Supportive Social Network

Correctly identifying feelings and developing healthy interpersonal relationships are important coping skills for individuals with c-PTSD. However, a supportive social network is also an important coping technique. The effects of c-PTSD may slow down the development of this network, as hypersensitivity can make new interpersonal interactions more difficult and create difficulties in maintaining these relationships. As a result, it can be helpful to seek out others who will support your needs to develop into a well-rounded individual.

A supportive social network involves finding individuals to interact with who understand and accept your needs while offering support and encouragement to build healthy relationships. Seeking out adults who will provide you with the skills you need to interact effectively, whether learning how to assert oneself or the right way to handle interpersonal situations, can be a helpful coping technique.

Seeking out a supportive social network can be very difficult in the context of c-PTSD. The hypersensitivity associated with this disorder may make people who struggle with it overreact to smaller social stressors. Finding adults who understand and respect your needs and providing them with healthy coping skills and support for their needs is one way that individuals with c-PTSD can gain skills and build their networks despite these difficulties.

A strong support system can help you feel less alone and provide a sense of belonging and validation. It can also provide practical help, such as assistance with daily tasks or emotional support during difficult times.

Here are some tips for building a supportive social network:

Join support groups: Look for local or online support groups focusing on c-PTSD or trauma. These groups can provide a safe space to share your experiences, learn from others, and build connections.

Seek positive relationships: Build relationships with people who support and validate you. Surrounding yourself with positive and caring people can help build self-esteem and promote healing.

Connect with family and friends: Don't hesitate to contact family and friends for support. Let them know what you are going through and what you need from them.

Volunteer or get involved in activities: Joining a club or volunteering for a cause you are passionate about can provide opportunities to meet new people who share your interests.

Consider therapy: A therapist can provide a safe and supportive environment to explore your experiences and emotions. They can also help you develop coping skills and strategies for building healthy relationships.

Remember that building a supportive social network takes time and effort. Be patient with yourself and others, and don't hesitate to ask for help.

CHAPTER 8

SMASH SELF-SABOTAGE: DARE TO EMBRACE CHANGE AND SUCCESS

This refers to overcoming self-destructive behaviors and thought patterns that hinder personal growth and success. Self-sabotage can manifest in various ways, such as procrastination, self-doubt, fear of failure, and negative self-talk. These behaviors and thoughts can prevent individuals from reaching their goals and fulfilling their potential. You must be willing to step out of your comfort zone, take risks, and pursue personal growth and success. It involves challenging self-limiting beliefs, overcoming fears and obstacles, and developing a growth mindset.

Overcoming self-sabotage and embracing change and success can be challenging, but it is essential for personal growth and well-being. It requires self-awareness, self-compassion, and a willingness to take action and persist despite setbacks.

Identifying Self-Sabotaging Behaviors

Self-sabotage is a cognitive process that starts by identifying your intentions and setting your goals. You will then develop strategies for overcoming obstacles and challenges that may impede you from reaching these goals. As you become more aware of your self-sabotaging patterns, you will become more aware of how they influence your thoughts and behavior, causing negative consequences.

Self-sabotage can manifest in various ways, including:

Procrastination is avoiding doing something you do not want to do by distracting yourself with other activities. It is an easy way to avoid negative feelings, but it can result in missed opportunities and stress. Many procrastinators believe they have a good excuse for not doing things (e.g., I have no time), but they are often mistaken. Procrastination is caused by anxiety, fear of failure or success, or lack of motivation. To overcome procrastination, you should acknowledge your negative thoughts that fuel this behavior and then challenge them until they become empowering beliefs (e.g., I will be able to handle the situation).

Fear of failure: this is common among people with low self-esteem but who work hard to compensate by putting in more effort. However, this may lead to burnout and stress, which can cause further procrastination. It would help if you challenged your fears by evaluating them and then determining whether they are realistic or exaggerated. Also, you must gain confidence and believe you can do something well despite your fears.

Negative self-talk refers to negative self-talk that you repeatedly repeat in your head (e.g., I am no good). You may also sabotage yourself by setting unrealistic goals (e.g., I should not make any mistakes). These self-talk patterns can lead to stress and anxiety. It would be best to challenge these thoughts by identifying them, analyzing them, and deciding whether they are valid or outdated.

Self-sabotage can also manifest in various actions, such as:

Stopping yourself from pursuing personal growth and success: for instance, not doing things you want to do (e.g., avoiding making a career change). Self-sabotage is often rooted in fear of failure or success. To overcome the fear of failure, you must gain confidence by building on your strengths and developing a growth mindset (e.g., take calculated risks and use new opportunities to your advantage).

Individuals with low self-esteem may also avoid personal growth because they believe they cannot handle success. They often feel they do not deserve it, which stops them from pursuing their goals. To overcome this self-sabotaging pattern, you need to practice self-compassion and engage in activities that boost feelings of well-being (e.g., reduce your stress and anxiety levels by practicing mindfulness).

Self-sabotage through self-injury: for instance, engaging in behaviors (e.g., burning yourself with a cigarette) or thinking about doing them (e.g., threatening suicide) to deal with negative emotions or experiences. These behaviors often compound stress and anxiety, which may lead to other self-sabotaging behaviors (e.g., substance abuse). Challenging these thoughts by identifying them, analyzing their validity, and deciding whether they are relevant or obsolete is important.

Self-sabotage can also manifest in various ways through various circumstances. For instance, it can occur when you do not work hard enough or put in the proper hours in your career, which can lead you to failure.

Other negative consequences of self-sabotaging behaviors include lost opportunities that could have provided greater happiness and satisfaction (e.g., opportunities to advance in a workplace or make new friends).

How self-sabotage can have negative consequences

Self-sabotaging behaviors and thoughts can have many negative consequences, such as:

Anxiety: you may become too stressed to do other things. You may feel restless or restless and get itchy. You may also feel overwhelmed by your thoughts and emotions. This often leads to uncontrolled impulses. For instance, you may feel the urge to make impulsive decisions that are not conducive to progress or success.

Impulsivity: impulsive behaviors take place without full deliberation, which means you cannot evaluate the options available. Impulsivity can have many negative consequences, such as worsening your self-esteem, poor decision-making, isolation (e.g., isolating yourself from others), or depression (e.g., feeling worthless).

Self-sabotage through substance abuse and addiction are examples of impulsive behavior. It would help if you learned to manage stress and anxiety by practicing mindfulness and reducing stress levels to overcome them.

Self-defeat is similar to giving up or failing in advance, which means you do not try because you do not believe you can succeed. Self-defeat often stems from low self-esteem, making one feel like one cannot succeed. However, they push themselves to work hard despite their fear of failure.

Discouragement occurs when you think your difficulties are insurmountable, so you give up and stop trying. You do not believe you can succeed because it seems too much for you. Sometimes, you may feel so discouraged that you stop doing anything and become hopeless.

If you feel like you are in a cycle of self-sabotage, it is important to identify the factors that influence it and learn how to overcome them.

Challenging Fears of Change and Success

Lack of action and inaction can be rooted in fear of change and success. The fear of change can come from the fear of leaving a comfortable situation, the inability to cope with new problems or uncertainty in new situations. To overcome this fear, you must:

Take risks: people who are afraid to take risks often wait until they are sure the outcome will be positive before taking action. However, sometimes, you need to take risks to get what you want; for instance, it could be your health insurance or the raise rate you need.

By taking some risks and not others, you may only feel like you have failed instead of suffering failure. For instance, in the above example, if you do not change your health insurance and raise rates to a level you are comfortable with, you will not feel like you have failed.

Learn to cope with change by learning new skills and building confidence: one way to do this is by learning new skills to manage well. For instance, it could be jobs that require team collaboration or communication skills. It can also develop your problem-solving abilities, which will help you deal with difficult situations effectively. These are some strategies for coping with adversity. By changing your perspective, you can boost your confidence which will help you do things that you fear. For instance, if you fear public speaking, knowing it is just a speech, not an actual performance, is a great way to overcome this fear.

Self-efficacy is the belief that you can do things well by saying "I can" or "I will." Self-efficacy can be developed by staying positive, spending time with people who support you, or learning new skills. These are some ways to increase self-efficacy.

Challenge and accept your fears: it may be as simple as challenging yourself enough to overcome or defuse them. By challenging your fears, you can think of ways to overcome and manage them effectively. For instance, practicing in front of the mirror or with a friend would be great if you are afraid of public speaking. By doing this, you can learn to feel more encouraged by the progress that you have made instead of the thought that "I cannot stand in front of people."

By accepting your fears, you can learn how to live with them instead of letting them control your actions and thoughts. For instance, if you are afraid of public speaking but do not want to give up on being a manager who has to give speeches all the time, see how well you take on this situation. When you start to see that you are not as afraid of it anymore and can start to get better at it, instead of trying to avoid it, your fear will soon disappear.

By overcoming your fears of change and success, you can feel more comfortable in changing situations and that the outcome could be better than what you have. You will learn to deal with and feel confident about those changes.

Challenging fears is a way to develop a growth mindset to accept new challenges and opportunities. By thinking positively and working on a solution, you can learn how to cope with change effectively, making you more successful overall.

Techniques for Overcoming Self-Sabotage

This general technique can be used whether you are trying to overcome self-sabotage or other challenges. It involves identifying your self-defeating thoughts and replacing them with more positive ones. While many thought patterns can lead to self-defeating behavior, there are ways to counteract these thoughts and replace them with a more positive attitude. The following is a list of methods for overcoming self-sabotage:

Identify why you engage in self-sabotage: it would be best to start by clarifying your reasons for feeling threatened, depressed, or disinterested in an activity. Once you have these reasons, you can work on identifying the behaviors that cause these thoughts and emotions.

It is also important to identify the thoughts that stem from self-defeat. For instance, a thought may be, "I will never be able to do this." Recognizing this thought as a self-defeat type of thought is the first step in overcoming it.

Admit your faults: it would be best to admit you are engaging in self-sabotage. By doing this, you will feel more empowered and able to change your negative thinking patterns.

Replace thoughts and feelings with positive ones: once you have identified your negative thoughts and feelings, think about ways to replace them with positive ones. For instance, a thought could be, "I am going to be just as good or better than anyone else." Controlling your thoughts and emotions will be easier with this thought in mind.

Set goals and follow through with them: it would be best to set specific goals and follow through with them. Examples include getting a raise, cleaning your apartment, or finishing that essay.

Focus on work: it is also important to focus on what you are doing right instead of what is wrong. For instance, when you get angry at someone or start thinking negatively, think about how you want the situation to turn out instead of focusing on the negative actions of others.

Reward yourself: it would be best to reward yourself for your efforts. By doing this, you will feel better about your progress instead of becoming discouraged.

Get enough rest: getting enough sleep and time out each day would also be a good idea. Doing this can prevent you from becoming stressed or angry, which will otherwise lead you to sabotage your efforts.

Get professional help: it is important to recognize when self-sabotage is causing more problems than the solutions you are trying to create. If you feel that your behavior impacts more than you, getting professional help may be helpful.

Remember, overcoming self-sabotage is a process that takes time and effort. Be patient with yourself and celebrate your progress along the way.

Embracing Growth and Progress in Recovery

Embracing growth and progress in recovery is the willingness to move beyond your comfort zone. Trauma recovery requires changing old thought patterns, behaviors, and beliefs that led you to experience flashbacks about your traumatic event(s). For this to happen, you need to be willing to change.

Growing and progressing can be tough at times. By embracing growth and progress in recovery, you can accept the challenging aspects of learning new coping skills, managing emotions, and learning how to problem-solve effectively. Instead of avoiding problems or expecting life and the world around you to change just how you want them to, always expect a change in yourself first. It would help if you were willing to learn and stretch yourself to a new way of living.

The following techniques will help you embrace growth and progress in recovery:

Identify and acknowledge emotions: Identifying the emotions triggered by your flashbacks or phobias is important. This will allow you to process the emotions instead of letting them control your actions.

Be willing to face challenges: when you are willing to move past your comfort zone, you will be able to understand the challenges presented by those changes. Doing this will reduce the chance of failing or faltering in these areas.

Be reflective about difficult situations: it is important to reflect on the difficult situations you are experiencing instead of just avoiding them or reacting impulsively. You can learn from your mistakes when you approach a situation from a reflective perspective.

Once you have made a mistake, be willing to learn from it and make changes in the future. By doing this, you will feel less threatened by failure and more empowered to try new things in life.

Being able to embrace growth and progress in recovery allows you to be more present in each moment instead of feeling stuck or stagnant. You will recognize your accomplishments and challenges, allowing for continuous improvement instead of being stuck in old thinking patterns that lead you nowhere.

Celebrating Your Achievements and Milestones

Achieving a milestone or achievement in recovery is a distinctive way to celebrate your progress. When you have achieved a goal or objective, it becomes easier to continue striving and achieving more positive changes in personal functioning. Reaching this point often helps you gain motivation and strength to move forward in the future.

Celebrating your achievements and milestones in recovery is an important part of the ongoing trauma recovery process. The following are some ways that you can celebrate these accomplishments:

Create a gratitude journal: it is beneficial to create a gratitude journal highlighting the positives you have experienced during your journey. For instance, you may want to write about the goals that you have achieved and the ways that your life has changed because of your trauma recovery plan.

Create a "bucket list": creating a bucket list of goals you want to achieve in the future would be beneficial. Doing this will make it easier to stay optimistic while focusing on what is possible instead of what is impossible.

Milestones: Celebrating every milestone you achieve during recovery is important because these signify a significant step towards healing and recovery.

Looking back: it would be a good idea to look back when times were tough and reflect on how far you have come since then.

Create a bigger picture: it would be useful for you to create a larger picture of your life, which includes different aspects such as mental health, occupational goals, spiritual well-being, financial stability, and physical health. By doing this, you can evaluate your progress and daily challenges.

Celebrating your achievements in recovery is important because they are major stepping stones toward becoming the person you want to be. Acknowledging these accomplishments can also help prevent self-sabotage and self-defeating behaviors.

Celebrating these milestones provides insights into where changes need to be made or areas that need improvement. It can also motivate you to continue striving towards your goals and objectives. You should know that it may be difficult to celebrate many of your achievements at first, but this is because change takes time.

You need to get help from others when you want to celebrate your achievements in recovery. It is okay for you to talk about how the changes that you have made allow for new opportunities and ways of living. A support network will also help you feel more supported and confident, which will help you reach your goals more easily.

CHAPTER 9

EMOTIONAL TIGHTROPE: BALANCE OVERSHARING AND AUTHENTICITY LIKE A PRO

This is a balancing act between sharing personal experiences and feelings with others while maintaining appropriate boundaries. Oversharing can make others uncomfortable or feel burdened while under-sharing can prevent meaningful connections from forming. Authenticity is important in building relationships, but knowing how to share safely and comfortably for all parties involved is important. Complex Post Traumatic Stress Disorder (C-PTSD) may make you feel vulnerable, fearful, and on a tightrope in your daily life. In this book, I'll show you how to balance your emotional tightrope to put you at ease and improve your relationships. This is a difficult skill to learn as your internal conflict about sharing and not sharing makes it hard for you to stay balanced, but I can help.

Understanding the Struggle to Find Balance in Relationships

We all have relationships where we share our feelings and thoughts to varying degrees. Some people are afraid to talk about their feelings, while others are so overly open that they bare their souls without care for how the other person feels. This is a human struggle, and it is normal to have an internal conflict about over or under-sharing your personal experiences. When you suffer from C-PTSD, this balancing act can become much more difficult because of the lingering internal chaos that's not immediately obvious to others.

You must recognize when you're feeling vulnerable or unsafe in a conversation so you can adjust accordingly. Relationships rely on trust and, ideally, will go smoothly if both parties communicate openly and honestly. Unfortunately, this can be difficult if you have issues with sharing yourself or if you're a person who overshares.

Finding balance in relationships can be difficult for anyone, especially those who have experienced trauma or have c-PTSD. People with c-PTSD may struggle to trust others or feel comfortable expressing their needs and boundaries, leading to a lack of balance in their relationships.

Here are some common challenges that people with c-PTSD may face in finding balance in their relationships:

Difficulty trusting others: People with c-PTSD may have difficulty trusting others due to experiences of betrayal or abandonment. This can make it challenging to build and maintain healthy relationships.

Fear of vulnerability: Vulnerability is essential to building and maintaining close relationships, but people with c-PTSD may struggle with vulnerability due to fears of rejection or judgment.

Difficulty setting boundaries: Setting and maintaining boundaries is important for healthy relationships. Still, people with c-PTSD may struggle due to fears of abandonment or a history of violating boundaries.

Tendency to overcompensate: People with c-PTSD may tend to overcompensate in relationships by being overly accommodating or putting their needs aside to please others.

To find balance in relationships, people with c-PTSD need to work on building trust, developing healthy boundaries, and practicing vulnerability in a safe and supportive environment. This may involve therapy, self-reflection, and communication skills training.

Strategies for Modifying Oversharing Behaviors

To learn how to filter oversharing behaviors without jeopardizing the relationship, it's important to recognize them and identify what triggers the behavior. Staying aware of your oversharing tendencies is important because they can lead to people developing a deeper distrust of you.

If you struggle with oversharing in your relationships, here are some strategies that may be helpful:

Set boundaries: Establish clear boundaries for yourself and others in your relationships. This can help you identify what you are comfortable sharing and what you would prefer to keep private.

Practice self-awareness: Pay attention to your feelings and emotions. Identify the triggers that may cause you to overshare and become more mindful of your communication.

Practice active listening: When conversing with others, focus on what they say rather than what you want to say next. This can help you stay present in the conversation and avoid oversharing.

Seek therapy: Consider seeking therapy to work through any underlying issues contributing to your oversharing behavior. A therapist can help you develop coping strategies and provide support and guidance.

Find alternative outlets: Consider finding alternative outlets for expressing yourself, such as journaling or creative projects. This can help you process your thoughts and emotions without oversharing in your relationships.

Remember that finding balance in relationships takes time and practice. Be patient with yourself, and don't hesitate to seek help if you need it.

Developing Healthy Boundaries and Emotional Regulation

Setting boundaries and regulating emotions is crucial to building healthy relationships. People with c-PTSD may struggle with these skills due to experiences or poor coping skills.

If you're struggling with setting and maintaining healthy boundaries, here are some strategies that may be helpful:

Identify your values and priorities: Understanding your values and priorities can help you set healthy boundaries and communicate your needs effectively.

Practice assertiveness: Learning to assert your needs and boundaries clearly and respectfully can help avoid oversharing or allowing others to overstep your boundaries.

Develop emotional regulation skills: Emotional regulation involves learning to recognize and manage your emotions healthily. This can include techniques such as deep breathing, mindfulness, or talking to a therapist.

Learn to say "no": Setting healthy boundaries often means saying "no" to requests or situations that do not align with your values or priorities.

Communicate openly and honestly: Being honest and clear about your needs and boundaries can help prevent misunderstandings or hurt feelings in relationships.

Practice self-care: Taking care of yourself physically, mentally, and emotionally can help you maintain healthy boundaries and manage your emotions effectively.

By developing these skills, you can find balance in relationships and avoid oversharing while remaining authentic.

Enhancing Interpersonal Skills and Communication

People with c-PTSD may struggle to communicate with others, especially in social situations or when initiating conversations. It can be difficult for people to communicate emotions and thoughts without feeling overwhelmed. Developing effective communication skills can help you communicate more openly and honestly in your relationships. Here are some strategies that may be helpful:

Focus on the other person: Paying attention to what others say can help avoid communication pitfalls or awkward situations.

Be open-minded: Approach interactions with an open mind to avoid arguments and conflicts that may arise due to misunderstandings or miscommunication.

Be aware of your tone and body language: Tone of voice, volume, and body language can affect how others perceive you in a conversation. Ensure your tone is friendly and inviting, and watch your body language for signs of discomfort or discomfort.

Avoid "shoulds": Avoid using "shoulds," such as "I should…" or "You should…" when talking to others. This can make it difficult for the other person to communicate their needs and boundaries.

Practice active listening: When conversing with others, focus on what they say rather than what you want to say next. This can help you stay present in the conversation and avoid oversharing.

Be authentic: Be yourself, include your own experiences and ideas, and be open with others about your emotions and needs.

Addressing these communication issues may be especially challenging for people with c-PTSD due to their tendency toward avoidance or silencing in relationships. A therapist can help you with these skills and support you toward a healthier relationship style.

Fostering Authentic Connections

Authentic connections are key to building healthy relationships. When you communicate authentically with others, you can develop trust and understanding by being honest about your needs and expressing yourself. Here are some strategies that may be helpful:

Express yourself clearly: Be honest about your own needs, feelings, thoughts, and beliefs in a clear, respectful manner.

Be comfortable being vulnerable: Expressing your emotions or sharing personal experiences can help others understand your feelings. Try engaging in activities where you're more likely to feel vulnerable, such as reading a book or journaling.

Be open and honest: Open communication allows people to see you at your best and understand who you are. Be open with others in the hopes they will be honest with you too.

Allow others to be vulnerable, too: Letting others share their thoughts, feelings, and experiences with you can help you understand them more and build trust in the relationship.

Seek out shared interests: Connecting with others who share your interests and passions can make it easier to build authentic relationships. Joining groups or clubs that align with your interests can be a great way to meet new people.

Practice active listening: Active listening involves fully focusing on the person you are communicating with and showing genuine interest in what they say. This can help build trust and create a deeper connection.

Be present at the moment: Being present during social interactions can help you fully engage with others and build authentic connections. This involves putting aside distractions and fully focusing on the person you are interacting with.

Practice empathy: Showing empathy involves recognizing and understanding the emotions of others. This can help build a deeper connection and foster a more meaningful relationship.

Fostering authentic connections with others takes time and effort, but it is an important part of healing and developing a sense of belonging. By practicing vulnerability, seeking out shared interests, practicing active listening, being present in the moment, and practicing empathy, you can build genuine relationships with others that can support your healing journey.

CHAPTER 10

BYE-BYE COMPARISON: HELLO SELF-COMPASSION AND PERSONAL GROWTH

It would help if you stopped comparing yourself to others and instead focused on developing self-compassion and promoting personal growth. Many people fall into the trap of comparing themselves to others regarding appearance, career success, relationships, or other areas of life. This can lead to feelings of inadequacy, low self-esteem, and even depression or anxiety. Instead, individuals can develop a more positive and fulfilling sense of self by focusing on self-compassion and personal growth.

Self-compassion involves treating oneself with kindness, understanding, and empathy. This means recognizing everyone has flaws and trying to be kind to oneself instead of overly critical. Personal growth involves setting goals, developing skills, and learning from mistakes to become the best version of oneself.

By letting go of comparison and focusing on self-compassion and personal growth, individuals can cultivate a healthier and more fulfilling relationship with themselves. This can lead to greater self-esteem, resilience, and overall well-being.

The Pitfalls of Constant Comparison

When individuals compare themselves to others, this can lead to feelings of inadequacy. This can be especially true when other people are doing better than they are or if they don't feel as confident or successful as someone else. One can become easily discouraged when comparing oneself to others because knowing what others are capable of is impossible. Comparing oneself with others also makes it more difficult for an individual to receive genuine compliments, which can be perceived as a hidden form of criticism compared to someone who truly cares for you. You may also worry about your shortcomings and how the rest of the world perceives them without feeling good about themselves.

Overall, constant comparison can lead to feelings of inadequacy and feelings of being worthless. This can be especially true if one is comparing themselves to others negatively, for example, thinking that they are inferior or not good enough. Comparing oneself with others may also lead to more self-criticism and depression.

When comparing oneself with others, one may feel like they don't have a lot of value because everyone else looks better or is doing better than them. It is important to remember that each individual has unique qualities and is unique in their own right; however, some do better than the average person at certain tasks.

Going about life with constant comparison can also lead to difficulty accepting compliments. This is especially true if one is comparing themselves to others negatively. Instead of enjoying the compliment, one may worry about how others perceive them and respond in a way that makes it seem like they don't believe it.

Constant comparison can make it difficult for an individual to feel good about themselves or receive help from others when needed. It can also lead to problems with self-criticism and depression.

Focusing on Personal Growth and Self-Compassion

They can accept help, support, and genuine compliments when you focus on yourself. This can be especially true when accepting compliments and positive feedback from others. You can feel a sense of accomplishment or gain confidence when receiving compliments or positive feedback from others.

In contrast, if an individual constantly compares themselves to others, it can be difficult to accept help from others or take the time to develop skills and personal growth; therefore, this may lead to feelings of inadequacy and feeling worthless.

By focusing on personal growth and self-compassion, individuals are more likely to accept genuine compliments, feel more confident in themselves, and feel a sense of accomplishment when trying to achieve goals.

It is important to recognize that each individual is different and has different strengths and weaknesses; however, one should also be proud of oneself when one tries to improve or develop skills. Individuals can feel good about themselves by focusing on personal growth and self-compassion.

Individuals may have greater overall well-being by focusing on personal growth and self-compassion. In contrast, constant comparison can lead to feelings of inadequacy, low self-esteem, depression, or anxiety.

Cultivating a Productive and Positive Mindset in Recovery

When trying to achieve sobriety or recovery, it is helpful to surround oneself with a community or group of people who support one another. This can be especially helpful when focusing on the positive and developing a sense of self-compassion and personal growth.

To begin, it can be helpful for individuals to find a comfortable environment free from judgment and criticism to foster positive support systems. For some individuals, this may mean joining an inpatient recovery center where they can focus on their recovery without having other distractions.

Cultivating a productive and positive mindset is crucial for individuals in recovery from c-PTSD. This is because it can be difficult to recover from trauma and develop a healthy sense of self when constantly comparing themselves to others.

With the right support system, individuals in recovery can learn how to accept help and support from others, develop genuine relationships built on trust, and cultivate a sense of self-compassion.

Here are some strategies to help cultivate a productive and positive mindset:

1. Set realistic goals and targets.

Setting realistic goals and targets can be especially helpful for individuals in recovery because it helps foster a sense of self-compassion and more confidence in what is possible. This does not mean that an individual should set unrealistic goals or targets; however, by setting realistic goals and targets, it can be easier to stay on track and achieve them when the time comes.

2. Develop feelings of self-compassion for one's struggles and weaknesses.

Developing feelings of self-compassion can help individuals recognize their struggles and weaknesses within themselves instead of focusing on the struggles or weaknesses of others. For some individuals, this may mean recognizing one's mistakes or failures and forgiving oneself. For others, this may mean recognizing failures or weaknesses in their relationships and changing these dynamics in the future. By developing self-compassion, individuals can feel more comfortable accepting themselves and more confident when changing their behaviors.

3. Recognize that each individual is different and that not everyone is the same.

Recognizing that each individual is different can help individuals feel okay about themselves despite the differences between them and other people. Therefore it can be helpful for them to develop a sense of peace within themselves when it comes to feeling better than or inferior to others compared to how they felt before starting recovery.

4. Forgive and move on from mistakes and failures.

Forgiving oneself for mistakes or failures can help individuals feel a sense of real personal growth. For example, suppose an individual was previously addicted to alcohol and failed to achieve sobriety. In that case, they can learn from these experiences, forgive themselves, and move forward in their recovery, knowing what to do differently in the future.

5. Accept compliments and positive feedback with grace.

Accepting compliments with grace can help individuals feel better about themselves because they can recognize their strengths instead of constantly feeling inadequacy due to self-criticism or constantly comparing themselves to others. When others accept compliments with grace, it helps them to feel a sense of satisfaction and accomplishment.

By developing an optimistic mindset and cultivating a sense of self-compassion and personal growth, individuals can feel better about themselves without negatively comparing themselves to others.

Strategies for Overcoming the Comparison Trap

The comparison trap is a common mindset that can negatively impact an individual's self-esteem and personal growth. Here are some strategies to overcome it:

When trying to overcome the comparison trap, it can be important for individuals to understand that they should not compare themselves to others and instead focus on improving their self-compassion and personal growth. By focusing on their prevention instead of what others are doing, individuals should feel better about themselves and have greater self-esteem and overall well-being.

By focusing on developing a healthy dose of self-compassion, an individual can set realistic goals and targets for recovery without having a constant comparison mindset. Setting realistic goals and targets makes it easier for an individual to stay on track with recovery because they do not need to compare themselves with others to feel good about themselves.

Focus on what one is doing right. By focusing on what one is doing right and noticing positive aspects of their behavior, individuals can feel better about themselves despite their shortcomings. For example, suppose individuals feel that they do not act like other people in recovery. In that case, it may be helpful for them to recognize how their behaviors are different from the other people in recovery that they see to see the positive aspects of their behavior. By focusing on how one's actions differ, an individual will not need to compare themselves with others and will feel better about themselves regardless of how they compare themselves.

Forgive oneself for mistakes and failures. Forgiveness can help individuals feel better about themselves regardless of what kind of mistakes or failures they have in their life. Suppose an individual fails at mediating or is addicted to alcohol. In that case, it can be helpful for them to focus on the aspects of their successful recovery instead of how they compare themselves with others who have failed to recover in the past. For example, suppose an individual is recovering from addiction and has not smoked for a year. In that case, it may be helpful for them to focus on how well they have acted toward other people instead of focusing on how well someone else acted in the past.

Remember that personal growth and self-improvement are a journey, not a destination. Embrace your unique path and focus on your growth and development.

Embracing Your Unique Journey and Successes

The comparison trap is a common mindset that can negatively impact an individual's self-esteem and personal growth. Individuals can overcome the comparison trap by developing a healthy dose of self-compassion and personal growth. By developing self-compassion, individuals will feel more comfortable accepting themselves without comparing themselves. Developing feelings of self-compassion helps individuals realize their successes in their recovery instead of focusing on failures in recovery so they can better focus on their personal growth goals. Focusing on personal growth goals helps individuals have greater self-esteem and self-worth.

Focusing solely on personal growth goals and successes gives one a greater sense of personal growth and self-esteem.

Be mindful of other people's successes and failures. Recognizing that others are doing better than you can help an individual feel less inadequate due to comparing themselves with others who have achieved better recovery behaviors than they have. If an individual notices how someone else is doing better at recovery than they are, it can be helpful for them to recognize their shortcomings or mistakes so they can learn from them and improve themselves in the future.

By focusing on what one is doing right in their recovery, individuals will feel better about themselves and have greater self-esteem. Feeling good about themselves will help them recognize how well they act in other areas of their life instead of focusing on how they compare themselves with others.

Greater personal growth is achieved when individuals focus on improving and developing healthy habits instead of focusing solely on accomplishments made by others. By developing a sense of self-compassion, individuals can overcome the comparison trap to focus on making positive changes instead of feeling better about themselves at someone else's expense.

CHAPTER 11

RISE FROM THE ASHES: GIG-WORK YOUR WAY TO SELF-SUFFICIENCY AND CONFIDENCE

Building confidence is never easy, especially when you are in the middle of a post-traumatic stress disorder episode or struggling to lift your self-esteem from rock bottom.

The trauma of PTSD affects our ability to read social cues and respond appropriately. This can lead to greater task difficulty, from simple messaging to relationships.

B.1 The Hopelessness, Helplessness, and Unemployment Trap

This is the feeling of complete and total hopelessness. To a survivor, there is no path forward.

Even though you have PTSD, you cannot live as if nothing happened to you. You cannot start over because it reminds you of how vulnerable your life was in the hands of that abuser or the threat of that trigger.

Unemployment can often lead to hopelessness and helplessness, making it difficult for individuals to see a way out of their current situation. This can be especially true for those who have experienced trauma or have mental health challenges such as c-PTSD.

The experience of unemployment can be quite challenging and overwhelming for many individuals, particularly those already struggling with mental health challenges. The sense of hopelessness and helplessness that comes with long-term unemployment can be especially difficult to overcome, leading to a cycle that can be challenging to break out of.

In some cases, individuals may feel stuck in a trap, unable to escape their situation. This can lead to a lack of motivation, self-doubt, and a sense of despair, making it difficult to take the necessary steps to find a new job or create a new path forward.

It's important to recognize that the experience of unemployment can be incredibly challenging and that it's okay to seek help if you're struggling. Many resources are available, including mental health professionals, job coaches, and community organizations that can provide support and guidance during this difficult time.

It's also important to remember that the experience of unemployment does not reflect your worth as a person. It can be easy to fall into the trap of believing that you're not good enough or that you've somehow failed if you're unable to find work. However, the reality is that many factors can contribute to unemployment, and it's not a personal failure.

If you're struggling with feelings of hopelessness and helplessness related to unemployment, reaching out for support and taking steps to care for your mental health is essential. This may include seeking therapy, connecting with support groups, practicing self-care, and staying connected to loved ones. With time and support, it's possible to break out of the trap of hopelessness and find a new path forward.

B.2 Cultivating Self-Sufficiency for Recovery

Learning how to be self-sufficient is crucial for recovery. We cannot expect others to fill the space in our life that our abuser once occupied.

It can be tempting to turn to others for validation, support, and help with the tasks we used to rely on our abusers for. However, this is not an effective strategy for recovery and can lead to greater feelings of loneliness and abandonment.

A great deal of self-care comes from knowing how to care for ourselves. This includes making decisions about our time, space, and relationships in a healthy way. Self-sufficiency means meeting your needs without depending on others or expecting them to fulfill your every need or desire.

During recovery, learning to take care of yourself this way and connect to the available resources is essential. It's also important to learn how to be secure in your decisions and how to set boundaries appropriately. If you're unsure what these things look like, it's a good idea to connect with a therapist to get support in making healthy choices.

The experience of self-sufficiency means that you can make decisions about your time, space, relationships, work, and other aspects of your life as an individual. It's possible to be self-sufficient without the help of others, and it's not necessary to rely on others for everything you need. Self-sufficiency does not mean you're in control of your life; rather, it means you have the self-awareness and ability to care for yourself. However, that may look. If you're struggling with issues related to self-sufficiency, make an appointment with a therapist and let them know what's happening.

B.3 Developing a Sense of Purpose and Direction

Recovery means feeling hopeful, and hopefulness can be difficult to achieve. Hopelessness can make it feel like there is no point in moving forward with recovery.

Many survivors, especially those who have experienced trauma and abuse, struggle with a lack of direction and purpose. They feel lost and unwilling to take control of their own lives. This experience of being stuck can lead to self-doubt and a feeling that there's not much point in moving forward for the survivor.

Thinking about what would help you move forward can be important if you're struggling with hopelessness. Consider what would help you feel hopeful about the future.

Many survivors struggle with finding a sense of purpose in their life, which can lead to a feeling that there's no point in moving forward with their recovery. It's crucial to remember that it's possible to imagine a brighter future, no matter how dark the present may feel. There are endless possibilities for your recovery and future, and it's unnecessary to wait until you've recovered before thinking about them.

If you can imagine your recovery, setting goals and taking steps toward achieving them can be easier. By thinking about your future, you're putting yourself in a position to take control of your life and move forward.

If you're unsure what you might want from recovery, it's a good idea to consider what would make recovery worth continuing. This can be different for every person, but it's important to commit to moving forward if there is something that you think is worth the work. Recovery can be challenging, and sometimes you want to give up or give in.

B.4 Strategies for Gaining Confidence and Employability

For individuals with C-PTSD, gaining confidence and employability can be particularly challenging. Many obstacles can stand in the way of building a career and a future, but there are also plenty of resources that can be helpful.

If you're struggling with confidence and employability, it can help you make specific goals. It's important to remember that the process of gaining confidence may take time, and it's natural for there to be setbacks along the way.

There are many ways to gain confidence and become more employable during recovery from C-PTSD. Some people find that they succeed best when they work with professionals who support them in their journey; others prefer to do it alone. Sometimes you'll need to try multiple strategies before you find what works best for you.

Here are some additional strategies that may be helpful:

Seek trauma-informed therapy: Working with a therapist specializing in trauma can help you address the underlying issues related to your C-PTSD, such as low self-esteem, fear of failure, and difficulty managing emotions. This can help you develop coping skills and increase your resilience, improving your confidence and employability.

Practice self-compassion: Individuals with C-PTSD may struggle with negative self-talk and harsh self-criticism. Practicing self-compassion can help cultivate a more positive and supportive inner dialogue, increasing your confidence and sense of self-worth.

Identify triggers and develop coping strategies: C-PTSD can be triggered by certain situations or experiences, making it difficult to navigate the job search process. Identifying your triggers and developing coping strategies can help you feel more prepared and in control when faced with challenging situations.

Consider accommodations: If you have C-PTSD, you may be eligible for workplace accommodations, such as flexible scheduling, noise-canceling headphones, or a private workspace. These accommodations can help you feel more comfortable and supported in the workplace.

Focus on your strengths: Individuals with C-PTSD may focus on their weaknesses or areas where they struggle. Focusing on your strengths and the things you do well can help you feel more confident and capable.

Build a support system: Having a supportive network of friends, family, or colleagues can be incredibly helpful in building confidence and employability. Consider joining a support group, contacting friends or family members for support, or networking with others in your field.

Remember, healing from C-PTSD and building employability skills is a process that takes time and effort. It's important to be patient and kind to yourself along the way and to seek support when needed. With time and effort, it is possible to increase your confidence and find a job that is a good fit for you.

B.5 Balancing Work, Relationships, and Self-Care for a Stronger Recovery

Recovery from C-PTSD can be difficult on both the individual and the relationships they surround themselves with. It's important to remember that recovery takes time.

Many people with C-PTSD struggle with different aspects of their recovery, and these issues can often get in the way of finding a job and building a healthy relationship. Balance is essential, but achieving full balance overnight is impossible.

Here are some helpful strategies for moving through these life transitions:

Set boundaries: It can be helpful to set limits when you feel overwhelmed by work, relationships, or self-care responsibilities. Your boundaries may include avoiding places, people, or responsibilities that are too much for you.

Talk with your friends and family: If you're overwhelmed at work, sharing your experience with others in a similar position can be helpful. They may offer support or advice on how to manage it.

Explore your motivation: It's important to ask yourself why you're struggling. Is it due to the stress of work? Is it about the quality of relationships? Is there something specific that is creating more stress for you? Being honest about why you're struggling can make all the difference in how successful your recovery will be.

Set realistic expectations: It's important to set realistic expectations for yourself in terms of what you can realistically achieve at work and in your personal life. This may mean adjusting your workload or schedule or communicating with loved ones about your needs.

Prioritize self-care: Prioritizing self-care is essential for maintaining mental and physical health. This may include exercise, meditation, therapy, hobbies, or time alone to recharge.

Communicate with loved ones: Communicating openly and honestly about your needs and boundaries can help you maintain healthy relationships while caring for yourself. This may mean setting boundaries around work or social obligations or being clear about when you need support or alone time.

Manage stress: Stress can be a major trigger for individuals with C-PTSD, so it's important to have strategies to manage stress when it arises. This may include deep breathing exercises, mindfulness meditation, or physical exercise.

Practice time management: Managing time effectively can help you balance work, relationships, and self-care. This may mean prioritizing tasks based on importance, delegating tasks to others, or creating a schedule that allows for adequate rest time.

Seek support: It's important to have a support system when managing recovery challenges. This may include seeking support from a therapist, support group, or trusted friend or family member.

Remember, recovery is a journey, and it's important to prioritize your well-being along the way. By setting realistic expectations, prioritizing self-care, communicating with loved ones, managing stress, practicing time management, and seeking support, you can create a balanced and fulfilling life that supports your recovery.

CONCLUSION

If you're struggling with Complex PTSD or just feeling stuck in life, there are steps you can take to get your sh*t together and move forward. It starts with acknowledging your past trauma and its impact on your present. This can be painful, but it's necessary to understand yourself and your triggers.

Not everyone with a history of trauma will end up with Complex PTSD. However, if you have limited your life experiences due to shame, self-blame, and flashbacks, there may be ways to reclaim your life.

It's also important to know that there are people who can help you heal and build the confidence to move into a more satisfying life. Getting support doesn't mean you've failed or are crazy; it just means you're willing to do what it takes to feel better.

Reread the exercises in this book, think about which would be helpful for yourself, and incorporate them into your routine. Once you've gained some insight, you can start to take action. Setting goals and prioritizing them can help you focus on what's important. But don't forget to break down those goals into smaller, manageable steps. Celebrate your progress, and don't beat yourself up for setbacks.

You're doing your best, and that's all you can do. It may be hard to believe, but some people can help you heal and learn to live a more fulfilling life. They have their scars, but they know what it's like to face the challenges of grief, depression, and PTSD. They've been there and done that, which makes them qualified to guide you into a brighter future.

Self-care is also crucial for healing and growth. This can mean different things to different people. Still, it often involves getting enough sleep, eating well, exercising, and engaging in activities that bring you joy—setting boundaries and saying no to things that drain your energy or trigger your trauma. Living with compassion, kindness, and empathy toward yourself is vital. It means accepting that you have been hurt and then moving on. But it also means forgiving yourself and others who've hurt you.

Take care of yourself and don't blame or shame yourself for past mistakes or mistakes that may happen in the future. People make mistakes but can learn from them, grow, and become stronger. It's unrealistic to think we can be the person we were before a trauma occurred. We can change for the better, but it always comes with pain and suffering.

You aren't alone. Whether you've been affected by Complex PTSD or have a family member who has, there's a lot of support to help you rebuild your life, learn to love yourself, and move forward.

Don't forget to reach out for support as you work on yourself. This can come from friends, family, therapists, support groups, or other resources. You don't have to go through this alone; asking for help is a sign of strength, not weakness.

If you're ready to move beyond your past trauma, consider connecting with someone who knows what it's like to heal from trauma. You can build a strong relationship and bond over your shared experiences. But it's also okay to go at your own pace, learn what you need and face the things that give you the most anxiety and discomfort.

Treat yourself with kindness, compassion, and empathy. You've been through a lot, but there are ways to heal from your trauma. It may take time, but you deserve the best life possible.

It's important to reflect on your progress and note any changes you've made. By defining your goals, prioritizing them, and breaking them down into smaller steps, you can start taking action toward achieving them. Acknowledging and working through any trauma or issues holding you back is also important. Through self-reflection and self-care, you can build a stronger sense of self and find the motivation to keep moving forward. Progress takes time and effort, but you can get together and live a fulfilling life with consistency and perseverance.

It would help if you tried to get the most out of this book. There is no way around it. This is not a quick-fix book that will make you feel better without any effort. Working hard at it is the most important thing for getting stuff done.

Feelings and emotions are emotions, but hard work gets things done. That's how life works, and there's no getting around it. It can be hard, but it can also be rewarding and enjoyable if you get out of your way and let yourself go through the process.

Dealing with PTSD can be difficult, and you may think there's nothing you can do about it. If you're struggling, everything will be okay soon, so don't make any drastic changes.

Instead, let yourself go through the process and use what you've learned to build a strong foundation for the future. You can't change the past; there's no need to think about it or dwell on it for too long. The sooner you move beyond your trauma and focus on the present and future, the better things will be.

There's a time to work through things, and there's a time to let go of all your problems. If you're still dealing with PTSD, this book you should consider reading as a helpful guide toward healing. It may be hard to believe now, but eventually, your past won't affect you as much as it does now.

To get the most out of this book, remember that it won't happen overnight. This is a real, proven treatment that works for many people. But not everyone who reads this book will experience healing and growth. The difference between those who heal and grow and those who don't is how much they apply the knowledge they gain from reading this book.

If you want to heal, it can be hard work sometimes and won't always be comfortable, but it will be worth it if you stick with it. If you don't feel like you're making progress right now, remember that progress takes time. You may not notice any changes immediately, but your life will eventually look different.

Don't give up on yourself because things aren't getting better immediately or as quickly as you like. Keep working on yourself and give your life to adjust. Doing the work needed to heal from your trauma is important because it will significantly impact the rest of your life.

There are a lot of things that can trigger your trauma and make you feel bad about yourself. Avoiding situations and people that remind you of the past will only lead to stress and anxiety.

Instead, use your strengths, skills, talents, and interests to help you rebuild a sense of self-worth and make the necessary changes for a better future. If you commit to taking care of yourself in every way possible, there's no limit on how far you can go.

You don't have to do this alone, either. No matter how big or small your problem is, some people want nothing more than to help you get through it. If you're willing to ask for help, you'll find many people who will listen and help you.

When it comes to healing, it helps to have a positive outlook on life. If you keep telling yourself that things can't get any better, they won't.

On the other hand, if you choose positive thoughts instead of negative ones, things will improve because your perspective on life changes as a result. It's hard to go through the healing process when you focus on what makes you feel worse about yourself or how bad your past trauma still affects your life today.

DESCRIPTION

Are you a sufferer of complex PTSD? This workbook will help you find ways to get yourself together with ten actionable exercises. You'll learn how to manage flashbacks, learn to cope with strategies, and have a clearer understanding of what keeps you from moving on.

This is an interactive and empowering resource that'll teach you how to deal with traumatic memories, find healthy ways of grieving, and take back control of your life. You'll find plenty of ways to cope with your strong emotions and regain balance.

Complex PTSD is also known as CPTSD, and it's a kind of PTSD that people often overlook. It's important to remember that everyone reacts differently to trauma. Many people can live through traumatizing events and never experience symptoms of PTSD. Those who do develop the condition may actually develop complex traumatic stress disorder instead of just regular PTSD, which makes it even more important to seek therapy right away.

Complex post-traumatic stress disorder affects millions of people and occurs after exposure to highly traumatizing events such as rape, abuse, natural disasters, or the death of a loved one. People who experience this type of PTSD may feel intense feelings of guilt, shame, and self-blame after their traumatic event. PTSD sufferers may feel like they are no longer in control of their thoughts and emotions, as these feelings become amplified to the point where they begin to control the individual.

This book covers

- Kicking the Numbing Habit: Ditch the Dependencies and Face the Feelings
- Therapeutic Trust: Building a Rock-Solid Relationship with Your Therapist
- Anchoring to the Now: Stop Time-Traveling and Embrace the Present

And much more

The ten exercises may seem difficult at first, but once you complete the workbook, you'll see how simple and effective it is. The exercises are designed to be done in order for all that comes along in your life - whether it be challenging events, therapy sessions, or even just day-to-day activities - they will help you learn how to deal with PTSD throughout your life.

If you are suffering from symptoms consistent with Complex PTSD, then this is the workbook for you. Additionally, if negative life events have caused you to dissociate from some of your memories or feelings, this book will help guide you through the steps necessary to begin processing them.

This workbook is for people who want to take back the power of their life. If you've struggled to cope with your overwhelming emotions and if you have found yourself dissociating from traumatic memories, then this workbook will show you what it means to get your sh*t together.

For those who have been affected by complex PTSD, this book is a resource that will show you practical ways to process the pain and heal yourself. If you've suffered from complex PTSD and if certain things back in the past have caused feelings of isolation and dissociation, then this workbook will help you learn to move past those painful experiences and start to find peace.

Printed in Dunstable, United Kingdom